THE STRUCTURE OF
BIBLICAL AUTHORITY

THE
STRUCTURE
OF
BIBLICAL
AUTHORITY

REVISED EDITION

by

MEREDITH G. KLINE

WILLIAM B. EERDMANS PUBLISHING COMPANY
Grand Rapids, Michigan

dedicated to
Cornelius Van Til

PREFACE

Ten years ago in the preface to *Treaty of the Great King* I commented on the importance of the rediscovery of the ancient treaty form for our understanding of the origins of the canon concept. Development of this theme waited, however, while attention was given to studies of the significance of the treaties for the interpretation of the biblical covenant concept itself and for the recovery of the meaning of the covenant signs of circumcision and baptism. Those studies eventually appeared as *By Oath Consigned* (1968).

My continuing primary interest in the relevance of the recent treaty investigations for theology moves on in the present volume from the doctrine of the sacraments to the doctrine of the Word. The initial concern with the canonical aspect of Scripture led inevitably to reexamination of the formal character of Scripture as such. "What is the Bible?" became a central question, and it receives here a somewhat distinctive answer, in line with the new direction taken in the formulation of biblical canonicity. Because of the limitations of the author's field of specialization the focus of these studies is on the Old Testament, but some suggestions are ventured for the extension of the main theses into the New Testament.

Part I consists of articles that were published in the following issues of *The Westminster Theological Journal:* XXXII, 1 (Nov. 1969), 49-67; XXXII, 2 (May 1970), 179-200; and XXXIII, 1 (Nov. 1970), 45-72. They have undergone revision and some expansion, especially the material of Chapter 2, in order to take account of the more recent literature. A much abbreviated version of parts of the articles will also be found under the title, "The Correlation of the Concepts of Canon and Covenant," in *New Perspectives on the Old Testament* (Waco, 1970), a volume of papers presented at the twentieth annual meeting of the Evangelical Theological Society in December 1968.

The first two chapters of Part II are taken from *Treaty of the Great King,* which is now out of print. These studies of the Decalogue and Deuteronomy are very closely related to the discussions in Part I and are frequently referred to there. Their republication here, while serving in general to keep them available, provides the reader of Part I with convenient reference.

Except for a little stylistic editing, these two chapters are reproduced unchanged, partly in the interests of preserving their character as introducing new applications of (what was when they were written) the freshly recovered knowledge of the ancient treaty form. It will be in order at this point, therefore, to indicate briefly how the ideas they introduced have fared in the intervening decade.

In general, a growing volume of studies has been pointing out the broad influence of the ancient treaties on the form of biblical revelation, while this development has been depreciated by some whose higher critical theories are undermined by it. As for the Decalogue in particular, some resist the identification of its form with the treaty pattern by reducing the correspondence to three documentary elements. This reduction is achieved, however, only by the devious technique of using the very documentary analysis of the Pentateuch that would be exposed by the new objective evidence of the treaty parallels as a scholarly phantasy in order to silence that evidence. The Decalogue is whittled down and isolated from its context, and thus half of the documentary and all of the accompanying ritual elements are eliminated which would otherwise demonstrate the thorough correspondence between the Decalogue and the treaties. Failure to recognize the parallel has also been due in part to disregard of significant features common to the Decalogue and the treaties, like the interspersing of sanctions with stipulations. And quite ignored has been that point of correspondence provided by my explanation of the two tables of the Decalogue as the duplicate treaty documents that were customarily prepared in covenant-making so that the suzerain and the vassal(s) might each have his own copy. Republishing of "The Two Tables of the Covenant" these ten years later is still timely, therefore, since it may (in effect) introduce a new consideration into the current discussion.

My identification of Deuteronomy as the text of a treaty, and specifically one in the classic pattern of the second millennium B.C., touched on a sensitive area and evoked a variety of reactions. Although there had been a general failure to recognize it, or say it, before the appearance of "Dynastic Covenant," the acknowledgment that Deuteronomy is a clear example of the treaty pattern is now common, even on the part of those who do not admit the facts in the case of the Decalogue. Since, however, the distinction between second- and first-millennium forms of the treaties has received considerable criticism, my identification of the Deuteronomic form with the earlier stage of that development has also met with resistance. In fact, the customary critical seventh-century dating of Deuteronomy has been supported by appeal to some points of close correspondence in detail, specifically in certain series of curses, with seventh-century Assyrian treaties. On this matter, I would mention at once that the existence of the distinction between earlier and later forms of treaties and Deuteronomy's use of the second-millennium form have been cogently argued by K. A. Kitchen, who had independently arrived at an analysis of the treaty structure of Deuteronomy practically the same as mine.

As for the similarities of a group of Deuteronomic curses to a section of curses in the later treaties, this is not adequate evidence to date even this particular material late, for the tradition of curse formularies extends far back into the second millennium B.C. Moreover, since the critics in question suppose that Deuteronomy developed over a period of time through a process of additions and modifications, they would be in no position to appeal to the presence of demonstrably seventh-century curse formulations (if there were such) as compelling evidence of a late origin of the treaty structure of the book as a whole.

Conservative criticism has all along been noting the lack of evidence that ancient Near Eastern documents were ever produced through an elaborate process of conflation of alternating sources in the way theorized by modern documentary speculation about the Pentateuch. More pointedly, treaty documents certainly did not grow by gradual accretion. They were produced whole for a particular occasion. Furthermore, inherent in their very structure was self-protection, in the form of document curses, against any subsequent alterations. Unfortunately, there seems to be a general unwillingness at present to face up to the obvious implications of the treaty identification of Deuteronomy to which form criticism has now led.

If it is once recognized that the Deuteronomic treaty must have been produced whole for a particular occasion, the pervasive orientation of the book to the situation of Israel in the Mosaic age and especially the central concern of this treaty with—of all things—the dynastic succession of Joshua, always awkward for advocates of a seventh-century origin of the book, become quite inexplicable for them.

Since the Deuteronomic researches of von Rad have been so prominent in the past and it was, accordingly, with them especially that my original article interacted, particular attention will be given here to his subsequent studies that have been published in his commentary, *Deuteronomy* (1964; Eng. tr., 1966). The comments that follow are taken from my review of that book in *The Westminster Theological Journal*, XXX, 2 (1968), 233ff.

The studies of the structure of Deuteronomy made by von Rad twenty-five and even thirty-five years ago remarkably anticipated what has subsequently been revealed by the publication of evidence as to the form of ancient treaties. He had recognized in Deuteronomy the pattern of a covenant renewal ceremony, and the more recent investigation of the treaties has made it clear that the pattern identified by von Rad was indeed covenantal. Yet, now that there is objective confirmation that his form-critical analysis was pointing in the proper direction he seems more embarrassed than gratified. Apparently the evidence would lead him farther than he is prepared to go. For it shows that his covenantal pattern was not just cultic but documentary. Furthermore, it discloses a more comprehensive structuring of Deuteronomy according to this documentary paradigm and at the same time testifies to an earlier date for the book in the overall integrity of its treaty form than von Rad's historical-philosophical predilections will permit him to accept. The ironic result is that von Rad's treatment of Deuteronomy today is as remarkably obscurant as it was brilliantly penetrant over two or three decades ago.

Given von Rad's assumptions, Deuteronomy could not be what it claims to be and what the evidence of the treaties confirms that it is. It claims to be a renewal of the Sinaitic covenant administered by Moses to Israel when transferring the leadership to Joshua. It claims, therefore, to be prophetic (in an anticipative sense) in its formulation of the stipulations as well as the sanctions of the covenant. In its stipulations it makes provision for the near future (when Jordan would have been crossed and Canaan possessed) and the more remote future (when a monarchy would have been established and God would have appointed a permanent location for the central sanctuary). In its sanctions it previews God's dealings with Israel for the next millennium down to their exile and restoration (to say no more). Where such phenomena appear, and they are of course pervasive, von Rad repeatedly asserts his presuppositional convictions, dogmatizing that the particular stipulation or sanction was formulated after the historical development it purports to anticipate. The whole second-millennium-B.C., Mosaic-Transjordanian origin attributed to itself by Deuteronomy is thus reduced to a fiction.

The problem for von Rad is to justify his persistence in giving methodological priority to his quasi-objective literary and form-critical observations in spite of the availability of solidly objective evidence which contradicts his conclusions by demonstrating the integrity and antiquity of Deuteronomy's literary form. Of course, that is not von Rad's reading of the situation. In fact, he still blithely asserts that the arrangement of Deuteronomy 4-30 "certainly cannot be explained as due to literary considerations" and that we must on the contrary "suppose that Deuteronomy is here following a traditional cultic pattern, probably that of the liturgy of a cultic festival" (p. 12; cf. p. 23). He is, therefore, content with continuing to support what is essentially his old position with the same old arguments. For example, opposing the unity of the book, he still appeals repeatedly to the alternating second person singular and plural forms, though admitting in more than one passage that the data are perplexing (i.e., his usual explanation of the plurals as belonging to an expansionist revision does not seem applicable), and, worse still, ignoring the objective evidence of the same kind of alternation within the indisputable unity of certain treaty texts.

A prominent contention in von Rad's form-critical assessment of Deuteronomy is that the trend towards exhortation, which he regards as "the real characteristic" of its presentation of the law (p. 19), reflects a history of homiletical embellishment of earlier cultic and legal traditions. He identifies the Deuteronomic preachers as Levites. Moreover, he observes a "pronounced warlike spirit" in the hortatory as well as legal parts and he explains this as a revival of the ancient holy war traditions, precisely locating the movement in the peculiar military-political circumstances of Josiah's reign following Sennacherib's invasion in 701 B.C. But while Deuteronomy thus "took effect" in Judah in the seventh century B.C., its place of origin, judging from other considerations like its concern with all Israel and its kingship provisions, must have been a sanctuary of northern Israel. As von Rad thus tries to take account of all the Deuteronomic data, which divorced from their proper Mosaic setting refuse to fit into any other one historical setting, his reconstruction becomes increasingly complex and uncertain. He is obliged to end his discussion with a series of unanswered questions about when and in what form Deuteronomy reached Judah from the northern kingdom, appending the conjecture that as a final stage in the process Deuteronomy was inserted during exilic times into the so-called Deuteronomistic historical work (embracing Joshua through 2 Kings), Deuteronomy 1:1-4:43 and 31-34 being the connecting ligaments.

In a later generation, when today's high priests of the higher critical gnosis are no longer venerated, this grotesquely complex explanation compounded of special theories within special theories will be recalled with a smile. Meanwhile, some criticism can already be heard of von Rad's failure to do justice to the evidence of Deuteronomy's correspondence to the legal-literary form of the ancient treaties. Thus, in a recent survey of the matter ("Deuteronomy—the Present State of Inquiry," *Journal of Biblical Literature*, LXXXVI, 3 [1967], 249-262), M. Weinfeld observes that "the structure of Deuteronomy follows a literary tradition of covenant writing rather than imitating a periodical cultic ceremony which is still unattested" (p. 253). He also finds it more reasonable to ascribe the work to a literary than a Levitical circle. He attributes it to the court scribes of the period of Heze-kiah-Josiah.

The oration character of Deuteronomy Weinfeld ex-plains as a literary device: programmatic speeches were placed in the mouths of famous persons to express the ideological views of the author (pp. 255f.). On this point von Rad comes closer to the truth. For while he too deems fictional the casting of Deuteronomy in the form of a farewell speech of Moses, he does at least formally integrate this feature with the covenantal elements in the book. He identifies the speech as an office-bearer's fare-well (cf. Josh. 23; 1 Sam. 12; 1 Chron. 22 and 29) and explains the presence of the covenant formulary within this and other such speeches by reference to the attested practice of renewing covenants when vassal leaders trans-ferred their office to a successor. Unfortunately, von Rad fails to recognize in the oration form the true explanation of the hortatory trend in the Deuteronomic treaty. This feature does not derive from Levitical preaching nor from a late literary circle of court scribes, but from the histori-cal circumstance that Deuteronomy is the documentary deposit of a covenant renewal which was also Moses' farewell to Israel. The element of parenesis already pres-ent to some extent in ancient treaties was naturally exploited to the fullest by Moses on that stirring oc-casion.

To acknowledge the presence of the treaty formulary only in miniature in this or that passage in Deuteronomy but not in the overall structure of the book involves a decidedly selective type of perception. For those who do perceive that Deuteronomy as a whole exhibits the treaty pattern, one fact demands more serious attention than it has hitherto received. Such treaties were sealed legal witnesses not subject to scribal revision. When changes in the covenant arrangement were required, that was accom-plished by preparing a new treaty, not by fictionally projecting the modified situation with its new terms within a bygone historical framework.

The third chapter of Part II below, "The Intrusion and
the Decalogue," is derived from an article which appeared
under that title in *The Westminster Theological Journal*,
XVI, 1 (1953), 1-22. In its present form it is condensed
and has had an overhauling, largely stylistic. It has been
included because of the relevance of its thesis to the
issues raised in Part I, Chapter 4.

To the editors of *The Westminster Theological Journal*
once again go my thanks for permission to publish in new
form materials originally presented on its pages. And to
Mr. Gary Pratico I would express my appreciation for his
kindness in preparing the indexes.

*   *   *   *   *

Cornelius Van Til stands as the prince of twentieth-
century Christian apologetics. He has had by far the most
profound impact on my own thinking of all my teachers.
His theological insight and prophetic witness have been a
conscience, if not canon, and his warmly human and
gracious godliness has been an inspiration for the life
which is in Christ Jesus. To turn a biblical phrase, may he
not regard the small estate of this book but only the
unbounded esteem and affection his servant, the author,
would express in dedicating it to him.

                                                   —M.G.K.

Hamilton, Massachusetts
November 1971

PREFACE TO SECOND EDITION

A new chapter (Part II, Chapter 4) has been added in this edition. It is a slightly revised version of an article due to appear in *The Westminster Theological Journal,* XXXVIII, 1 (1975). Continuing the theme of the covenantal New Testament (cf. pp. 68ff.), it follows up the suggestion that the gospels are covenant witness documents (p. 72). In the process, an exception emerges to the earlier statement that the several New Testament genres are not the same as the major Old Testament genres (p. 71).

Apart from the addition of this new chapter, the present edition leaves the first edition virtually unchanged.

—M.G.K.

September 1975

CONTENTS

PART ONE

CANON AND COVENANT

INTRODUCTION

The history of the formation of the Old Testament canon, particularly its beginnings, has been relatively neglected. Elaboration of the subject along genuinely Scriptural lines has been forestalled by the preoccupation of orthodox scholarship with the critique of aberrant current reconstructions. These modern approaches have concentrated narrowly on the aspect of a final definitive "limitation" of the canon, and consequently the attention of all concerned—the heterodox reconstructionists and their orthodox critics alike—has been directed for the most part to developments, whether actual or alleged, in the last pre-Christian and the earliest Christian centuries.

Discovery of the relevant evidence from this period in the library of the Qumran community has been hailed as the most significant new light on the Old Testament canon and has engendered reassessments. However, no really radical revisions of the characteristically modern viewpoint have emerged. Accounts of the subject in the latest editions of the standard Old Testament introductions produced by that school adhere to the same theological posture and the same general historical positions found in the old handbooks on the canon from the end of the last century.

Fohrer, for example, in his revision of Sellin's work, asserts that the "formation of the Hebrew canon in the strict sense did not take place until the time of Sirach and his grandson" in the second century B.C., being "completed between 100 B.C. and A.D. 100."[1] This delimiting of a sacred collection of scriptures is said to have been a dogmatic decision reached by way of reaction to threats to legalistic Judaism from apocalypticism, the Qumran faction, and above all from Christianity. More precisely, the process of canon formation supposedly involved three separate stages, each with its own collection of books— the law, the prophets, and the writings. Fohrer traces the prehistory of the process to Josiah's reformation, to which he attributes "the introduction of the Deutero- nomic law as an obligatory norm" for all of life, further affirming that "in the period immediately following, Deu- teronomy practically became the first holy scripture."[2] All this will be recognized as the long-current critical tradition concerning this subject.

The familiar hypothesis that the Old Testament canon recognized in Alexandria was broader than that accepted by Palestinian Judaism has indeed been challenged from within the modern school. Not, however, on the grounds that the evidence for a broader Alexandrian-Septuagint canon is inadequate, but, on the contrary, that there is evidence for a similarly broad attitude in Palestine itself during the first century A.D., particularly in pre-70-A.D. Judaism.[3] The new theory contends that during the days of Jesus and his apostles no closed canon of Jewish scriptures had been defined, whether Palestinian or Alexandrian, and that the Western church accepted a broader collection while Judaism of the late first century

[1] E. Sellin and G. Fohrer, *Introduction to the Old Testament* (tr. D. E. Green; Nashville, 1968), p. 486.

[2] *Ibid.*, p. 484.

[3] Thus, A. C. Sundberg, Jr., in *The Old Testament of the Early Church* (Cambridge, 1964); "The Protestant Old Testament Canon: Should It Be Re-examined?", *Catholic Biblical Quarterly*, XXVIII (1966), 194-203 (part of "A Symposium on the Canon of Scrip- ture" by Roman Catholic, Protestant, and Jewish scholars, pp. 189-207); and "The 'Old Testament': A Christian Canon," *Catholic Biblical Quarterly*, XXX (1968), 143-155.

A.D. settled for a narrower canon. And the conclusion is then drawn that Roman Catholics and Protestants should be able to concur on the Christian (or ecclesiastical as versus Judaistic) Old Testament canon. This is certainly congenial to the ecumenical tide, but it may well sound startling to many Protestant ears. Nevertheless, this thesis too is only a variation on the usual theme, working as it does with a conception of canon in which human decision is decisive and confining itself in general to the historical era centering around the activities in the school of Jabneh in the late first century A.D.[4]

A necessary service has been performed by those who have exposed the false theological premises of the modern approach to the canon and its misreading of the historical developments, as expressed particularly in the theory of a threefold "canonization" of the Old Testament.[5] The orthodox critique has rightly observed that this approach, by attributing to the voice of the community the determination of canonicity, fails to do justice to the character and claims of the Old Testament as word of God. The formation of the canon, rather than being a matter of conciliar decision or a series of such decisions with respect to a preexisting literature, was a divine work by which the authoritative words of God were through the mystery of inspiration inscripturated in document after document, the canon being formed by the very appearance of these God-breathed scriptures.

[4] On the extreme exaggeration of the significance of these discussions, see J. Lewis, "What Do We Mean by Jabneh?", *Journal of Bible and Religion*, XXXII (1964), 125-132.

[5] Cf. L. Harris' review of some of the issues in the *Bulletin of the Evangelical Theological Society*, IX, 4 (1966), 163-171, esp. p. 170, and X, 1 (1967), 21-27, esp. pp. 22ff. For a critique from quite a different point of view of the traditional modern notion of successive canonization in three stages of law, prophets, and writings, conceived according to the Massoretic arrangement and with the law as the foundation and controlling perspective in the development, see J. C. H. Lebram, "Aspekte der alttestamentlichen Kanonbildung," *Vetus Testamentum*, XVIII (1968), 173-189.

Fully justified also has been the criticism that the whole historical reconstruction of a threefold formation of the canon is, on the one hand, bound up with a thoroughly distorted overall picture of the chronological emergence of the Old Testament books, while, on the other hand, this threefold development hypothesis does not mesh with the dates its own advocates assign to the origin of several specific books. Furthermore, in the approach under criticism the nature and significance of evidence like that from the Septuagint, the Qumran community, the New Testament, the Jabneh school, and the early church have been seriously misconstrued, while the testimony of Josephus has been so minimized as to be practically ignored.[6]

In effect, the orthodox critique reveals that these current historical reconstructions deal scarcely at all with the history of the formation of the Old Testament canon, as they purport to do, but almost entirely with its epilogue, that is, with a late phase of the recognition of the boundaries of that canon in the postformative period. The real history of the Old Testament canon's formation—a millennium-long history—largely antedates even the era relegated in these treatments to the "prehistory" of the canon.

Along with the performance of this apologetic-critical function, orthodox scholarship has addressed itself to the more positive study of the canon. Efforts in this direction, however, have been largely concerned with the proper formulation of Scriptural canonicity in the dogmatic categories of the Bible's own objective self-authen-

---

[6] Cf. Lecerf's trenchant analysis of the modern critical methodology with its pedantic exaggeration of unimportant details, its polemical neglect of the decisive facts, and its illogical contention that the Old Testament canon in the Reformed confessional sense did not exist in the time of Jesus and his apostles because the Old Testament canon in the modern critical sense was, allegedly, a creation of Talmudist Judaism (*An Introduction to Reformed Dogmatics* [London, 1949], pp. 337ff.).

tication as word of God and the Holy Spirit's internal
testimony to the Word, and the relation of both of these
to individual faith and the church's sealing attestation to
the Word. The more precise delineation of biblical canonicity requires that it be perceived as fully as possible in its
specific historical character, and much remains to be
done along these lines.

It is then with the subject of the actual history of the
formation of the Old Testament canon that the present
study will begin. Attention will be given particularly to
the origins of the canon and its formal Near Eastern
background. The attempt will be made to arrive at a
specifically and authentically historical conception of the
matter, and thereby to make some contribution in the
area of prolegomena to Old Testament canonics.[7] It will
emerge, we believe, that for purposes of reappraising the
Old Testament canon the most significant development in
the last quarter-century has not been the Dead Sea scroll
finds but discoveries made concerning the covenants of
the Old Testament in the light of ancient Near Eastern
treaty diplomacy.[8]

Tracing the historical origins of biblical canon, though

---

[7] Dealing with the New Testament canon, H. Ridderbos (*The
Authority of the New Testament Scriptures* [Philadelphia, 1963],
pp. xif.) writes in a similar vein: "It is therefore a mechanical
isolation of the revelatory character of the Scripture, if the latter is
regarded in abstraction or if it is derived solely from formal
statements of its authority. The significance of Scripture and the
nature of its authority is properly delineated only if it is closely
related to the history of redemption. . . . Our investigation simply
seeks to delineate more sharply the essence of Scripture, and the
nature of its authority within the cadre of the history of redemption."

[8] N. B. Stonehouse expressed the judgment that no aspect of
Scriptural revelation was more basic or illuminating than its covenantal character (*Revelation and the Bible* [ed. C. Henry; Philadelphia, 1958], p. 76). He drew attention to the covenantal-
revelational features of divine sovereign enactment and of manifestation at decisive moments in history.

it is done for primarily positive purposes, will be found to have as a by-product a certain apologetic value as well. For twentieth-century critical versions of the formation of the Old Testament canon, in adhering faithfully to the nineteenth-century evolutionistic reconstructions, have accepted the latter's central assumption that the canon concept was late in dawning on the Israelite mind. And when that assumption is scrutinized in the light of the phenomena of pre-Israelite canonical documents, especially when account is taken of the ancient historical-literary data that reveal canon to have been the correlate of covenant, it becomes increasingly evident that what is being passed off in current canon studies as ancient history is essentially modern fiction.

Chapter One

FORMAL ORIGINS OF BIBLICAL CANON

Ancient Near Eastern Canonical Documents

The formal roots of biblical canon are discernible in the literature of the Bible's background. Of the several varieties of ancient texts that might be characterized as canonical the most important is the treaty document. For steadily increasing knowledge about the nature of the covenants by which international relationships were governed in those days has demonstrated a formal analogy between them and the Sinaitic and other divine covenants of Scripture.[1]

In these treaties an overlord addressed his vassals, sovereignly regulating their relations with him, with his other vassals, and with other nations. The central role played by the treaty tablet in which the covenant was customarily inscripturated is attested by the fact that the preservation of these tablets was at times made the subject of a special document clause in the text of the treaties. Moreover, as such a clause would stipulate, copies of the text, duplicates of which were prepared for all the parties

[1] The present writer has discussed the matter in *Treaty of the Great King* (Grand Rapids, 1963; hereafter, *TGK*) and in *By Oath Consigned* (Grand Rapids, 1968; hereafter, *BOC*).

concerned, were to be deposited in the presence of a god, carefully guarded, and periodically read publicly in the vassal kingdom.[2] In its formal features the canonical aspect of the biblical covenants (and of the Old Testament in general) was thus already clearly present in these international treaties.

Of particular importance for identifying the roots of canon in the covenant is, of course, the practice that called for drawing up the suzerain's authoritative words in writing.[3] Besides the separate document clause cited above, another indication that the written text of the treaty was integral to covenant administration is the special references to the tablets occasionally found in the treaties, describing the tablets themselves or significant details in their history. Thus, reference is made to the extraordinary material of a tablet: the tablet of silver that Hattusilis III made for Ramses II and the iron tablet inscribed by Tudhaliyas IV for Ulmi-Teshub. It is recorded that a treaty was written at such and such a place and in the presence of named witnesses. It is stated by a suzerain that he wrote the tablet and gave it to a vassal, just as, in the case of God's covenant at Sinai, Israel's heavenly Sovereign inscribed for them the tables of stone. Mursilis II mentions the tablet which was made by his father for a vassal but was later stolen, and he then relates his own writing, sealing, and delivering of a second tablet. According to the Hittite treaty with Sunassura, the transferal of his allegiance from the Hurrians to the Hittites, that is, the abrogation of one covenant and making of another, was effected by destroying the old treaty tablet and preparing a new one.

[2] Cf. V. Korošec, *Hethitische Staatsverträge* (Leipzig, 1931), pp. 100f.

[3] Cf. W. Beyerlin, *Origins and History of the Oldest Sinaitic Traditions* (tr. S. Rudman; Oxford, 1965), esp. pp. 55ff. Note, too, the combination of $kôt^eb\hat{\imath}m$ with $kôr^et\hat{\imath}m$ in the covenant ratification of Nehemiah 10:1 (9:38).

A feature of the covenant tablets of peculiar significance for their canonical character is the inscriptional curse, or what we may call the canonical sanction. The tablet was protected against alteration or destruction by making such violations of it the object of specific curses. This protective documentary curse was not exclusively a feature of treaties but was employed in various other kinds of texts such as commemorative and funerary inscriptions, votive inscriptions, like those on temple gate-sockets,[4] and law collections like those of Lipit-Ishtar and Hammurapi; it was most elaborately formulated on the *kudurru*'s.[5] Wherever it is found the inscriptional curse is somewhat stereotyped in content. This is so both in respect to the techniques envisaged by which the text might be defaced or removed and with respect to the divine retribution threatened as a deterrent to any contemplating such transgression.

From the treaty of Tudhaliyas IV with Ulmi-Teshub comes the inscriptional imprecation: "Whoever . . . changes but one word of this tablet . . . may the thousand gods of this tablet root that man's descendants out of the land of Hatti."[6] Similarly in Suppiluliuma's treaty with Niqmad of Ugarit anyone who changes any of the treaty words is consigned to the thousand gods. The treaty of Suppiluliuma with Mattiwaza states that the vassal's duplicate of the tablet has been deposited before the deity and is to be read at regular intervals in the presence of the vassal king and his sons, and then pro-

[4] Cf. S. Gevirtz, "West-Semitic Curses and the Problem of the Origins of Hebrew Law," *Vetus Testamentum*, XI (1961), 137-158.

[5] On these see further below. Cf. D. R. Hillers, *Treaty-Curses and the Old Testament Prophets* (Rome, 1964), pp. 11, 86; and F. C. Fensham, "Common Trends in Curses of the Near Eastern Treaties and *Kudurru*-Inscriptions Compared with Maledictions of Amos and Isaiah," *Zeitschrift für die alttestamentliche Wissenschaft*, LXXV (1963), 155-175.

[6] See D. J. McCarthy, *Treaty and Covenant* (Rome, 1963), p. 185.

ceeds: "Whoever will remove this tablet from before Teshub . . . and put it in a hidden place, if he breaks it or causes anyone else to change the wording of the tablet— at the conclusion of this treaty we have called the gods to be assembled . . . to listen, and to serve as witnesses." The invocation of a lengthy list of gods follows, with a reiteration of the purpose of their presence, and finally the curses on violators of the treaty and blessings on those who observe its injunctions. The sanctions begin: "If you, Mattiwaza, . . . do not fulfil the words of this treaty, may the gods, the lords of the oath, blot you out. . . ."[7] Continuing this tradition in the first millennium B.C., Esarhaddon stipulated concerning the tablet of the treaty oath with its dynastic and divine seals: "You swear that you will not alter it, you will not consign it to the fire nor throw it into the water . . . and if you do, may Ashur . . . decree for you evil."[8] And Barga'ayah cursed with death under torment anyone who boasted: "I have effaced these inscriptions from the *bethels*."[9]

The way in which the content of the treaties and the treaty tablet itself merge in the charge to guard it and in the conjoined curses against offenders reveals how closely identified with the idea of suzerainty covenant was its inscripturated form. And the inviolable authority of these written tablets, vividly attested to by the document clause and, especially, the documentary curse, sufficiently justifies our speaking of the canonicity of these treaties.

Along with the treaties there were other ancient documents that contained authority-laden directives and thus possessed in a broad sense a canonical quality. Even though the treaty form was the particular canonical genre

[7] See A. Goetze's translation in *Ancient Near Eastern Texts* (ed. J. B. Pritchard; Princeton, 1950), pp. 205f. (hereafter, *ANET*).

[8] See D. J. Wiseman, *The Vassal-Treaties of Esarhaddon* (London, 1958), p. 60.

[9] Sefireh II, C; cf. *TGK*, pp. 43f.

adopted as nucleus for the biblical revelation, it is well that we should be aware of this wider formal background of the Bible as canonical document. One such type of document was the professional prescription; examples would be the Egyptian medical papyri,[10] or magical incantations and cultic formulae. The authorship of such spells and rites, moreover, was attributed in Mesopotamia and Egypt to various gods, like Ea and Thoth.[11] Another category was the "letters of gods" addressed to Assyrian kings.[12] Another type would be the documents issuing from royal chancelleries, like edicts and laws. There were also the royal land grants witnessed to by the *kudurru* stones, which in general concept and literary tradition have much in common with the state treaties.[13]

[10] The authority of a prescription was commonly traced to its derivation from a canonical exemplar, an ancient document, particularly one found in a temple. The prescription might then be described as "what was found in writing under the feet of [the deity]," i.e., under the immediate guardianship of the god's image. The concept and terminology here parallel the practice of enshrining copies of treaties, as was stipulated in their document clause. The remedy might even claim to be a divine revelation. Thus, one papyrus reads: "This remedy was found in the night, fallen into the court of the temple in *Koptos,* as a mystery of the goddess, by the lector-priest of this temple." For this translation and sample texts of these prescriptions see J. A. Wilson's treatment of them in *ANET,* p. 495.

[11] See W. G. Lambert, "A Catalogue of Texts and Authors," *Journal of Cuneiform Studies,* XVI (1962), 59-77, esp. pp. 72f.

[12] Cf. A. L. Oppenheim, *Ancient Mesopotamia* (Chicago, 1964), p. 280.

[13] See L. W. King, *Babylonian Boundary-Stones and Memorial-Tablets in the British Museum* (London, 1912), pp. viiff.; and F. X. Steinmetzer, *Die babylonischen Kudurru (Grenzsteine) als Urkundenform* (Paderborn, 1922), pp. 95ff. On other royal grants, cf. M. Weinfeld, "The Covenant of Grant in the Old Testament and in the Ancient Near East," *Journal of the American Oriental Society,* XC, 2 (1970), 185. Weinfeld identifies such grants as promissory covenants, so distinguishing them from the obligatory covenants formulated in the treaties.

The *kudurru* inscriptions were written on roughly oval-shaped stones and on stone tablets, the former serving as public monuments and the latter as permanent private records. They were copied from original deeds on clay tablets, the records of royal grants of land and, occasionally, of related privileges. Along with the boundary description and, usually, the list of witnesses to the transaction copied from the original deed, the *kudurru*'s had engraved on them divine symbols and curses against anyone who would contest the title or molest the stone inscription. Other reliefs found on the stones depict in various combinations the figures of the king, the recipient, and a deity. These additional features were clearly intended to place the private property and other rights of the owner under divine protection. The *kudurru* pillar set up in the midst of the property thus confirmed the recipient's title to it and protected his land from encroachment.

Treaties and *kudurru*'s alike have, as already noted, inscriptional curses,[14] violations of both being threatened with the vengeance of the gods who are pictorially represented on these documents, as well as being invoked in the imprecatory clauses. In the case of both the *kudurru*'s and the treaties the identity of the physical tablets or pillars merges with the stipulated arrangement to which they witness. Further, it has been suggested that there is a legal analogy between these two types of texts.[15] For in the relationship defined by a treaty the tributary country was the property of the great king, and thus the treaty which he had enshrined in the land of the vassal was virtually his *kudurru* pillar (or better, his *kudurru* tablet), setting his legal claim to that territory within the sacral sphere for its enforcement.

A somewhat different legal analogy results if the

[14] On this parallel in detail compare, for example, Esarhaddon's treaty (lines 410ff.) with the characteristic *kudurru* curses.

[15] F. C. Fensham, *op. cit.*, p. 158.

kudurru is considered from another perspective, not as a property claim but as a royal charter granting property to a faithful subject. This aspect is especially pronounced in the *kudurru*'s that provide title to privileges beyond land. An interesting example is the *kudurru* which records the charter given by Nebuchadnezzar I granting to the cities of a faithful captain of his chariotry new political freedom and exemptions from various revenues and impositions of the military.[16] These benefits bestowed on cities are of the type symbolized by the *kidinnu*, the divine emblems set up in a public gate of the city and, like the *kudurru*'s, placing the privileged territory under divine oversight.[17] The analogy to this in the treaties is most evident in those treaties that included territorial guarantees and other special privileges for favored vassals; these, too, had the force of royal grants. Particularly in their geographical section with its list of cities and boundary descriptions these treaties remind us of the *kudurru*'s.[18] This *kudurru*-like feature is not missing in the case of biblical treaties. Indeed, they are very much concerned with a royal (here, divine) land grant and guarantee. This element, already prominent in the Abrahamic covenant, is resumed in the earliest renewals of covenant revelation in the days of Moses (e.g., Exod. 3:8, 17; 6:8); it finds mention in the Decalogue's sanctions (Exod. 20:12; cf.

[16] See L. W. King, *op. cit.*, pp. 29ff.; and, for other examples, pp. 96ff. and 120ff.

[17] Oaths were sworn by the *kidinnu*. See further W. F. Leemans, "*Kidinnu*, un symbole de droit divin babylonien," in *Symbolae van Oven* (Leiden, 1946), pp. 36-61; cf. A. L. Oppenheim, *op. cit.*, pp. 120ff.

[18] A good example of a treaty where *kudurru*-like territorial guarantees are prominent is that of Tudhaliyas IV with Ulmi-Teshub. It contains a detailed geographical section, and then toward the close, near the inscriptional curse, the treaty is identified in terms of the borders which the suzerain declares he has set, given, and inscribed on an iron tablet. For another example, see the comments on the treaty deed from Alalakh in *TGK*, p. 23.

Deut. 5:16, 33ff.) and pervasively in the Deuteronomic treaty; and it is a governing motif in the Book of Joshua, to trace it no further. Of interest in this connection are the stones triumphantly erected on Mount Ebal in the midst of the land possessed according to Yahweh's covenantal charter. These stones were designed, it would appear, to serve as something of a treaty and *kudurru* combined in a memorial pillar (see Deut. 27:2ff. and Josh. 8:30ff.).[19]

A further resemblance of a literary sort that the *kudurru*'s bear to the treaties is seen in the presence in some of them of an historical prologue. One such was the *kudurru* granted by Nebuchadnezzar I, cited above. Its historical section describes vividly the exploits of the captain-grantee and his legal negotiations leading to the awarding of the royal charter. In this extolling of the subordinate party and his services as the basis of the grant this historical prologue differed from those in the treaties of the second millennium B.C.; for the latter were devoted to magnifying the suzerain for his benefactions. Nevertheless, this literary feature is so significant an element in the pattern of the treaties (and, indeed, is of such interest for the broader question of the origins of historiography) that the mere presence of an historical prologue of any kind in the *kudurru*'s is noteworthy. And it apparently does point to a close interrelationship in the development of the treaties and the *kudurru*'s as kindred legal genres.

We may round out this comparison of these two kinds of royal, canonical documents with the observation that the extant *kudurru*'s date from the fourteenth to the seventh centuries B.C. and the major extant treaties belong to very much the same period. So, too, do the beginnings and the great formative era of the Old Testament canon.

---

[19] The copies of the Sefireh treaty were inscribed on steles.

Adoption of the Canonical Treaty Form

Our survey has indicated that canonical genres of various kinds can be identified among the documents that constitute the literary background of the Bible. One of these, the international treaty, proves to have special relevance for our understanding of the canonicity of the Bible inasmuch as it influenced to a remarkable extent the formal shaping of the Scriptures. Indeed, the very oldest Scripture, the Decalogue given at Sinai, was in treaty form, as was the Deuteronomic document, which summed up and sealed the earliest, Mosaic stratum of Scripture.

At Sinai, and again in the plains of Moab, the administration of Yahweh's lordship over Israel was solemnized in ceremonies of covenant ratification. Through Moses, his covenant mediator, the Lord God addressed to his earthly vassals the law of his kingdom. His authoritative treaty words, regulative of Israel's faith and conduct, were inscripturated on tables of stone and in "the book." Both these deposits of covenantal revelation accorded closely in their formal structure and ceremonial treatment with the ancient treaties, not least with respect to those documentary features of the treaties that provided the justification for our describing them as canonical.

Thus, the particular series of distinct sections constituting the classic treaty pattern supplied the documentary structure of both the Decalogue and Deuteronomy.[20] The duplicate tables of the covenant written at Sinai reflect the custom of preparing copies of the treaty for each covenant party.[21] In due course provision was made at Yahweh's direction for the Sinaitic covenant tables to be preserved inviolate in the ark of the covenant and for the Deuteronomic document to be kept by the ark in the sanctuary, permanent witnesses there to the

[20] Cf. *TGK*, pp. 14ff., 28ff.
[21] *Ibid.*, pp. 17ff.

covenant, and this deposition of them was in accord with the regular custom of enshrining treaty documents. [22] The directions for the deposition of the Mosaic treaties are given in the documentary type of clause which is closely associated in the extrabiblical treaties with the inscriptional curse, the brand-mark of canonicity (see Deut. 31:9-13, noting also 10:2 and Exod. 25:16, 21; 40:20). And the inscriptional curse itself also appears in the treaty beginnings of the Bible. In the midst of a passage in Deuteronomy that summarizes the entire treaty and is permeated with the covenant sanctions of the God who revealed himself in fire at Horeb, Moses warns: "You shall not add to the word which I command you, nor take from it; that you may keep the commandments of Yahweh your God which I command you" (Deut. 4:2; cf. 27:2ff. and Josh. 8:30ff.).

The literary tradition of the inscriptional curse, or canonical sanction, continues through the Scriptures. One reflection of it is the account of Jehoiakim's destroying of the scroll that contained the words of covenant sanctions spoken by God through Jeremiah (see Jer. 36). This account, like the inscriptional curses, concerns itself with the topics of the method employed to destroy the document and the curse visited on this offense. Moreover, the similarity extends to the use of fire in the act of destruction and to the pronouncing of curses on both the person and the property of the king, and particularly to the specific curses of the cutting off of his descendants and the casting out and exposure of his corpse.[23] Continuing down into the New Testament the canonical imprecation appears climactically in the Revelation of John. "I testify to every one who hears the words of the prophecy of this book: If any one adds to them, God will add to him the plagues described in this book, and if any one takes away

[22] *Ibid.,* pp. 19f.; cf. Beyerlin, *op. cit.,* pp. 57f.

[23] For parallels in treaties and *kudurru*'s, see Fensham, *op. cit.,* pp. 161ff., and Hillers, *op. cit.,* pp. 68f.

from the words of the book of this prophecy, God will take away his share in the tree of life and in the holy city, which are described in this book" (Rev. 22:18f.; cf. 1:3). While recognizing the reference to the Apocalypse, we cannot fail to appreciate the appropriateness of these sanctions to canonical Scripture as a whole.

To sum up thus far, canonical document was the customary instrument of international covenant administration in the world in which the Bible was produced. In this treaty form as it had developed in the history of diplomacy in the ancient Near East a formal canonical structure was, therefore, available, needing only to be taken up and inspired by the breath of God to become altogether what the church has confessed as canon. And that is what happened when Yahweh adopted the legal-literary form of the suzerainty covenants for the administration of his kingdom in Israel.

It is necessary to insist constantly that the Scriptures, whether the Mosaic covenant documents, which constituted the nuclear Old Testament canon, or any other Scripture, are authoritative—uniquely, divinely authoritative—simply in virtue of their origin through divine revelation and inspiration. Certainly, then, their authority as such is not to be accounted for by looking beyond them elsewhere. As divinely authoritative revelation, documentary in form and with unalterable content, they possess the essential components for a definition of canon properly conceived. Nevertheless, it is legitimate to inquire into the precise literary brand of canonicity in which God was pleased to cast his authoritative words, for this is an altogether different and purely formal matter. In this respect biblical canonicity does have an earthly pedigree. And what has become clear is that it was the treaty brand of canonicity inherent in the international treaty structure of the Mosaic age that was adopted by the earliest Scriptures along with the treaty form itself. Biblical canonicity shows itself from its inception to be of the lineage of covenantal canonicity.

The beginnings of canonical Scripture thus coincided with the formal founding of Israel as the kingdom of God. In the treaty documents given by Yahweh at the very origins of the nation Israel, the people of God already possessed the ground stratum of the Old Testament canon. Only by resisting the accumulating evidence can the modern critical dogma that the concept of canonical document did not emerge until late in the development of Israelite religious thought be perpetuated and "histories" of the formation of the Old Testament canon continue to be erected upon it.

Anachronistic Modern Canon Theories

Old Testament scholarship is, to be sure, for the most part unwilling to accept the biblical witness to the origins of the Decalogue and Deuteronomy in the days of Moses, except in some radically qualified sense. Some also would oppose the acknowledgment made by many that the Decalogue exhibits the Hittite treaty pattern. The picture is further complicated by critical hypotheses like that of von Rad rejecting the original integral relation of the Sinai-covenant tradition to the exodus tradition.[24] But even the holding of such viewpoints has proved compatible with consent to the judgment of the great majority who have now been obliged to repudiate Wellhausen's arbitrary recasting of historical sequence by which the covenant idea was made out to be a late outgrowth of prophetic thinking. Very few now fail to recognize the presence of the covenant in the pre-

[24] For a helpful recent critique of this hypothesis, see H. H. Huffmon, "The Exodus, Sinai, and the Credo," *Catholic Biblical Quarterly*, XXVII (1965), 101-113. The counter observations of P. B. Harner in "Exodus, Sinai, and Hittite Prologues," *Journal of Biblical Literature*, LXXXV (1966), 233-236, do not meet the issue. Cf. J. M. Schmidt, "Erwägungen zum Verhältnis von Auszugs- und Sinaitradition," *Zeitschrift für die alttestamentliche Wissenschaft*, LXXXII (1970), 1-31.

prophetic history of Israel's life and thought, and the tendency is to respect the evidence that traces covenant as far back as Israel can be traced.

It is evident, then, that an unrecognized tension has developed within the dominant school between its altered thinking about covenant and its unaltered, nineteenth-century thinking about canon. It will hardly do to continue to claim that the concept of canonical Scripture was an innovation of the late prophetic era and at the same time to admit that the covenant concept was a formative factor in Israel's literature in preprophetic times. For where there is divine covenant of the classic Old Testament kind there is divine canonical document.

Quite apart from consideration of the covenantal dimension of the Old Testament, the critical timetable for the formation of the canon has become increasingly problematic because of the higher dates now being assigned to various parts of the Old Testament. The difficulty becomes most pointed in the case of law materials,[25] where the aspect of authority is prominent. While it has been acknowledged that the Israelites at a relatively early time recognized certain written laws as divine revelation, the meaning of this for the history of the canon concept in Israel has been obfuscated.

Referring explicitly to the sanctioned status of the enshrined Deuteronomic law, Fohrer protests: "This does not yet imply a collection of sacred scriptures, and certainly not a process of canonization, because new law codes came into force down to the time of the Holiness Code and P. Not until Ezra's reformation, which stabilized the law, did the period end when a new law with divine authority could come into being."[26] This is, in-

[25] See the remarks of W. F. Albright on the antiquity of Mosaic law in *Yahweh and the Gods of Canaan* (London, 1968), pp. 149-159.

[26] *Op. cit.*, p. 483. Sometimes the Josianic lawbook episode is said to be the earliest instance of canonization. In endorsing this view, C. H. Gordon stresses the element of permanence in the

cidentally, another example of how hypotheses concerning the time of composition or redaction of the various books or parts thereof have dictated the shape of theories of canon formation. But Fohrer's protestations also betray an obscurant reluctance to reconsider the traditional critical posture on Old Testament canonization in the face of recalcitrant data. The force of admitted facts is escaped by making subtle adjustments in the definition of canon which arbitrarily elevate the secondary and accidental to essentials, while minimizing what is actually essential.

According to Fohrer's tailoring of the canon concept, canonical law-scripture did not exist until law-scripture ceased to be produced. On this redefinition, canonization becomes the closing of the sacred list on a particular literary species. There is then no beginning, no process to canon formation, only a point of completion—or a series of such points if the whole Old Testament is under consideration. In this approach, the community's act of endorsement is, of course, substituted for God's act of inspiration as the critical element in the creation of the canon. But more than that, the human act of endorsement which is equated with canonization is so qualified that writings could be regarded as divinely authoritative community rules without being necessarily canonical.

nation's adoption of a written, legal guide on that occasion. Cf. *The Ancient Near East* (New York, 1965), pp. 247f. R. H. Pfeiffer, working with similar premises, finds it impossible to date the canonization of the law so early; he points to the cultic activities of the Elephantine Jews as evidence of the noncanonical status of Pentateuchal law long after 621 B.C. See his *Introduction to the Old Testament* (New York, 1941), p. 57. And if one is thinking of the role of Pentateuchal law within Judaism, any claim of permanent adoption of the Josianic lawbook is invalidated by the last two millennia of Judaism without priest, altar, or sacrifice. Gordon's own recognition of this is implicit in his further assertion that the stage of canonical Scripture, which succeeded an earlier stage of guidance by oracle, has itself given way to a third stage: the interpretation of Scripture (*op. cit.*, p. 248, n. 12).

Canonization of the law awaited the termination of the period when new divine codes might come into being. Why? Was it that the envisaged new codes might not simply supplement but conflict with and abrogate divine laws already in hand, so that the authority of these present laws and Israel's endorsement of them might prove to have been only temporary? Might the Deuteronomic laws, for example, have to be changed or set aside, in spite of the fearful inscriptional curses protecting them? But why, then, would these old laws have later been canonized along with the new code precisely when they ceased to be normative? Such in any case is the curious way it actually happened, if one is to follow Fohrer in his total understanding of the matter. For the modern documentary partitioning of Pentateuchal law on which Fohrer's whole discussion rests does, of course, view the several law "codes" as in serious conflict with one another. Hence, strangely, the earlier laws did not become canonical until they were contradicted and eclipsed by the latest laws![27] Furthermore, for anyone who accepts the New Testament as canonical, would not the logic of Fohrer's redefinition of canon compel the conclusion that Old Testament law did not really become canonical until it was superseded by the final divine revelation in the new covenant? For the New Testament, too, has its revelation of law, its new commandment, its new mandate for a new organization and a new world mission for the community of the new covenant. Therefore, for Fohrer on his own definition of canon to allow (as he does) that the divine law became stabilized as Old

[27] Another undigested qualification introduced into Fohrer's definition is that the closing of the canon involves a standardizing of the process of textual transmission. Hence, though he allows that the law was stabilized in Ezra's reformation, he judges that a comparison of the Massoretic and Septuagint texts shows that the text of the law (or Pentateuch) was not yet fully determined in Ezra's day, and he concludes that the Pentateuch did not even then have canonical character (*op. cit.,* p. 484ff.).

Testament law before Christ and became canonical independently of the divine revelation of the new law of Christ's kingdom is to assume an un-Christian stance; however unintentionally, it implicitly denies that the New Testament is a new revelation with divine authority.

A somewhat different approach emerges in Noth's influential study of Pentateuchal laws.[28]   In his ingenious but contrived reconstruction Noth distinguishes between validity and canonicity. The shift to canonicity he locates in the postexilic period in connection with an alleged absolutizing and universalizing of laws whose legal validity was hitherto regarded as confined within the particular political constitution of Israel's amphictyonic confederation. This misinterpretation of the situation results to no small extent from Noth's misconstruing the nature and role of the covenant in the life of Israel and in the broader history of redemption.

But instead now of criticizing in detail this or that proposed redefinition of canonicity, let it suffice to make an observation about the general tactical state of affairs. The whole attempt to salvage the modern hypothesis of a late origin of the Old Testament canon by resort to new specialized definitions of "canonization" suggests that the scholars concerned have lost sight of the course of canon studies in the last century. One receives the impression that the determinative role of the Wellhausenian mold in the development of that theory has been forgotten and that its current promoters are consequently unaware that they have removed the original rationale of the theory from under themselves by their own significant reversals of Wellhausen.[29]

[28] *The Laws in the Pentateuch and Other Essays* (tr. D. R. Ap-Thomas; Edinburgh and London, 1966), pp. 1-107; the original form of the treatise in view appeared in 1940.

[29] That much can and should be said, even if one finds apropos M. Smith's exposure of the pseudo-orthodox (as he calls them) who imagine, or at least declare, themselves far more liberated

More especially, as has been indicated above, what is now known and commonly acknowledged about covenant in ancient Israel has rendered obsolete the inveterate critical thinking about Old Testament canon formation. The theory of a process of canonization beginning in the postexilic era, if not considerably later—whether a threefold process or otherwise, whether assuming a more extensive Alexandrian canon or following an approach like Sundberg's—is a grotesque distortion of the historical facts, a Wellhausenian anachronism on a millennial order of magnitude.

Conclusion

The origin of the Old Testament canon coincided with the founding of the kingdom of Israel by covenant at Sinai. The very treaty that formally established the Israelite theocracy was itself the beginning and the nucleus of the total covenantal cluster of writings which constitutes the Old Testament canon. While exposing the prevalent critical histories of the formation of the canon as the anachronistic fictions they are, orthodox Old Testament scholarship should also set to work on the biblical-theological task of delineating the real history of that process. When that is done and the relevant historical realities of ancient covenant procedure are brought to bear, the formation of the Old Testament canon will be traced to its origins in the covenantal mission of Moses in the third quarter of the second millennium B.C., providentially the classic age of treaty diplomacy in the ancient Near East.

Our conclusion in a word, then, is that canon is inherent in covenant, covenant of the kind attested in ancient international relations and the Mosaic covenants

from Wellhausen than they actually are. Cf. his "The Present State of Old Testament Studies," *Journal of Biblical Literature,* LXXXVIII, 1 (1969), 19-35, esp. pp. 25f.

of the Bible. Hence it is to this covenant structure that theology should turn for its perspective and model in order to articulate its doctrine of canon in terms historically concrete and authentic. It is the covenant form that will explain the particular historical-legal traits of the divine authority that confronts us in the Scriptures.

COVENANTAL BIBLE

Granted that biblical canonicity is in its beginnings covenantal, what of the Old Testament beyond the original Mosaic documents which are clearly couched in the classic treaty form? And what of the New Testament? Can the conclusions we have reached concerning the covenantal identity of biblical canon in its origins be justifiably extended to the whole Bible? Are all the Scriptures covenantal?

Covenantal Old Testament

It is, of course, the common Christian practice to refer to each of the two main divisions of the Bible as a "testament." In the case of the Old Testament there is ancient, even biblical, precedent. The apostle Paul speaks of the Israelites' reading of their Scriptures as a reading of "the old covenant" (2 Cor. 3:14). Whether he had in view the Pentateuch only or the entire Old Testament,[1] he plainly identifies Scripture in an extensive sense with covenant. Similarly, in a passage in 1 Maccabees, where the

---

[1] In the context (v. 15) Paul uses "Moses" apparently as an equivalent of "the old covenant," but "Moses" here, like "law" elsewhere, possibly denotes the entire Old Testament.

Scriptures collectively are called "the books of the law,"[2] an individual book of the Scriptures is referred to as "a book of the covenant" (1:56f.).

The aptness of the broad identification of the pre-Messianic Scriptures as "the covenant" or "the old covenant" will be perceived if the Old Testament's comprehensive witness to itself is accepted at face value. The human dimensions of the Old Testament are to be duly appreciated, but it is supremely important that we apprehend in faith the Old Testament's claim that God is its primary author. If we do, we will see the Old Testament as more than an anthology of various types of literature produced by a series of authors across a span of centuries. We will understand that it all issued ultimately from the throne room of Israel's heavenly King and that all its literary forms possess a functional unity as instruments of Yahweh's ongoing covenantal oversight of the conduct and faith of his vassal people.

We may come to the same understanding of the Old Testament by viewing it not directly in its ultimate issuance from its invisible heavenly source but in its immediate earthly derivation from the Israelite community. For all Israel's life, cult and culture, the latter in both the private-family and public-kingdom spheres, stood under the covenant rule of Yahweh. A peculiar significance was imparted to the whole by Yahweh's presence in the midst as God-King. His covenantal dominion, exercised from the nation's cultic center, the royal site of the theophanic presence, claimed Israel's life to its full circumference.

___

[2] For the comprehensive use of "law" to cover the whole Old Testament see Matthew 5:18; Luke 16:17; John 10:34; 12:34; 15:25; Romans 3:19a; and 1 Corinthians 14:21. For the use of "the law and the prophets" in the New Testament and Qumran texts as a designation for the entire Old Testament see R. L. Harris, "Was the Law and the Prophets Two-Thirds of the Old Testament Canon?", *Bulletin of the Evangelical Theological Society*, IX (1966), 163-171. The categories of law and prophets themselves had definitely covenantal connotations.

And because the cultic and cultural structures of Israel which were the immediate *Sitz im Leben* of the various parts of the Old Testament were thus so thoroughly covenantalized, it follows that all the inspired literature deriving from and related to that cult (like ritual legislation and hymns) and associated with that culture (like civil law, national history, diplomatic messages of prophets, and instruction of sages) served the covenant and inevitably bore its stamp.

Examination will further show, we believe, that the particular covenantal functions performed by the various parts of the Old Testament canon within the life of Israel stand in close relationship to one or another element in the Mosaic treaty documents. The several major kinds of literature—history, law and wisdom, prophecy and praise—as they are employed in the Old Testament all function as extensions (free and creative to be sure) of some main section or feature of the foundational treaties. The functional extension may be by way of administrative or judicial application or by way of didactic or confessional elaboration. But in each case a special relationship can be traced between the function and a particular element of the treaty documents, and thus a literary dimension is added to the functional in our identification of the Old Testament in all its parts as a covenantal corpus.

Our thesis is then that whatever the individual names of the several major literary genres of the Old Testament, as adopted in the Old Testament their common surname is Covenant. To display this fully would be the task of the discipline of Old Testament canonics. What follows is just a brief survey of some of the most salient data, but hopefully sufficient to substantiate the thesis.

Law

With regard to the legal material in the Old Testament, Noth observes that "it is not really self-evident that in a document of the faith, such as the Old Testament—a Holy Writ—there should stand laws which deal not only with cultic affairs but also with everyday social life."[3] And yet, while the problem of the origin of the law has been thoroughly discussed, the question concerning "the grounds and circumstances of the very presence of the law within the Old Testament at all" has received scant attention.[4] Whatever the merit of Noth's answer, it is to his credit that he insists that there is here a question which must be faced.

On the understanding of the Old Testament as a covenantal corpus, the presence of its legal materials is readily explained; for the stipulations imposed by the suzerain were a central element in ancient treaties. Those Old Testament laws contained in documentary units like the Decalogue and Deuteronomy which have the treaty form obviously find their explanation as treaty stipulations. But the other Pentateuchal laws are also set in a covenantal context. This context may be rejected as secondary in modern subjective reconstructions, but in the objective Pentateuchal setting in which they come to us these laws are presented as elaborations of the treaty obligations laid upon Israel as Yahweh continued to speak to them through the covenant mediator Moses.

The laws recorded in Exodus 20:22-23:33 are specifically identified as "the book of the covenant" (Exod. 24:7; cf. 4). The fact that this covenantal collection of laws deals with matters moral and ceremonial, civil and cultic,[5] individual and corporate, is indicative of how all

[3] *The Laws in the Pentateuch and Other Essays,* p. 10.

[4] *Ibid.*

[5] Note especially the interweaving of cultic with moral obligations (e.g., Exod. 22:20, 29ff.; 23:12ff.). Another explicitly covenantal promulgation of cultic-ritual law is found in Exodus 34:10ff. These laws are not to be equated with the text of the covenant tablets whose renewal is recorded in this context (Exod. 34:1ff., 28) and then regarded as a "cultic decalogue," but they are set forth as the words of God's covenant (Exod. 34:10, 27).

Israel's life fell within the purview and under the regulation of Yahweh's covenant with them. If the recognition that the Old Testament is a covenantal body of literature accounts for the presence of laws in it, the comprehensive scope of Yahweh's covenantal interest and claims will explain the wide variety of those laws, regulating as they do Israel's life in all its spheres and dimensions.

The distinctly covenantal orientation of the sizeable segment of laws dealing with the cultus becomes evident when it is observed that in Israel the cultus absorbed various vital features of covenantal administration which elsewhere were not cultic but matters of state. The uniquely religious nature of the Yahweh-Israel covenant naturally and necessarily transformed the political into the cultic. Though adapted from the model of man-with-man covenants, this was a covenant of God with men. The international treaties were indeed conceived of as having sacred sanction; the gods were involved as witnesses and enforcers of the covenants, the documents of which were accordingly deposited in their sanctuaries. But in Yahweh, God of Israel, the role of divine witness-avenger merges with that of covenant overlord. Yahweh is Israel's covenant suzerain; Israel's covenant lord is the Lord God.[6]

Hence, in the world of this covenant the palace of the great king is one and the same as the sanctuary of the vassal's God. Hence, too, the covenant ratification rites coalesced with the system of cultic sacrifice.[7] The custom-

[6] Cf. *TGK*, pp. 19f.; *BOC*, p. 92 with n. 14. It is the merging of the roles of covenant suzerain and divine witness-avenger in Yahweh that explains, too, the otherwise legally strange coalescence of plaintiff with witness-judge in the covenant lawsuit (on this lawsuit, see below under *Prophecy*). A special cultic liturgy need not be assumed as the setting in which the covenant lawsuit form arose.

[7] Cf. *BOC*, p. 18. The peace offerings gave expression to cordial relationship in the covenant bond. Cf. R. Schmid, *Das Bundesopfer in Israel* (Munich, 1964). See also Beyerlin, *op. cit.*, pp. 65ff.;

ary annual appearances before the suzerain to fulfill the tributary obligations of the treaty took the cultic form in Israel of the three required annual pilgrimages to Yahweh's sanctuary-throne to present offerings.[8] The covenantal character of these festivals is accented by the Deuteronomic stipulation that the treaty be read every seventh year at one of them, the Feast of Tabernacles. This periodic public reading of the text, which is a vassal obligation found in the international treaties too, was assigned in Israel to cultic officials (Deut. 31:9ff.).[9]

Another example of an elsewhere noncultic area of vassal obligation that became cultic in Israel is the requirement to render military assistance to the suzerain. This duty is heavily stressed in ancient treaties, and it assumes a place of considerable prominence in Yahweh's covenant with Israel (cf., e.g., Exod. 23:23f., 32f.; 34:11ff.). It takes on here the urgency of a mandate to engage forthwith in a program of conquest in the name of their Lord. It is a war of Yahweh, Israel's God, and therefore a holy war. Its object, according to the explicit emphasis in the Mosaic treaties, is the obliteration of the cultic installations and devotees of the idol-gods of Canaan and the establishment of Yahweh's cult in the midst of his sanctuary-kingdom.[10]

Other aspects of the covenant-cult in Israel may be mentioned. The sacrificial system of the cult was a means of making amends for offenses against the treaty stipulations and, in general, it was through Israel's participation in the cult that they most immediately experienced the covenant as a personal relationship with the Lord God.

commenting on the ratification of the Sinaitic covenant, he speaks of "the covenant-cult."

[8] Cf. *TGK*, p. 92; and D. R. Hillers, *Covenant: The History of a Biblical Idea* (Baltimore, 1969), p. 76.

[9] Cf. *TGK*, pp. 20, 135ff.; and Baltzer, *Das Bundesformular* (Neukirchen, 1964), pp. 91ff.

[10] Cf. *TGK*, p. 32.

On the other hand, infractions of ceremonial requirements at the individual level were grounds for excommunication from the covenant community (e.g., Lev.
17:4), and at the national level abuse of the cult is cited
by the prophets as a cause for the severance of the
covenant relationship. The covenantal nature of Israel's
cult gives a peculiar significance to the depositing of
Yahweh's treaty at the cultic center, so that the presence
of the tables of the covenant in the ark in Israel's sanctuary may be said to epitomize the coalescence of covenant
and cult in Israel.

Stipulations regulating the conduct of one vassal in
relation to another are not common in the political
treaties. We do, however, find the general principle that
the vassal was to be a friend to the suzerain's friends
(particularly, then, to fellow vassals) as well as an enemy
to his enemies.[11] The vassal's conduct in this intervassal
area was thus an aspect of his covenantal relation to his
suzerain. Agreeably, in the biblical laws governing the
relationship of the Israelite to his neighbor there are
indications that these obligations are related to the Israelite's vertical-personal involvement with Yahweh, his God,
and that they are, therefore, to be classified not with the
usual law collections of the other nations but with covenantal stipulations.[12] These indications may be of various kinds; for example, the familiar enforcement of the
obligation to show kindness to servants and the needy by
appeal to Yahweh's deliverance of Israel from bondage
(see, e.g., Deut. 5:15; 15:15; 24:18, 22) or by the re-
minder that Yahweh is the avenger of the oppressed poor
(see, e.g., Exod. 22:27; 23:7; Lev. 19:14); or the ground-
ing of the demand for holiness on the principle of follow-

[11] Of special interest here is the series of identical treaties of
Mursilis II with three of his vassals forbidding each to fall out with
the others. Cf. Genesis 12:3; 27:29; Numbers 24:9.

[12] Cf. *TGK*, pp. 17, with n. 12, and 25ff.

ing after Yahweh, who is holy (see, e.g., Lev. 11:44f.; 19:2; 20:7, 26).

Another important way in which Old Testament law differs from the ancient law collections and exhibits its covenantal nature is that it legislates for the corporate life of Israel. The treaties were, of course, concerned with the vassal kingdom corporately. Their stipulations dealt with the vassal kingdom's dynasty and boundaries, with its national policy in war and peace, and appended to them were sanctions national in scope. So also Pentateuchal law prescribes for the Israelite community a system of government with priests and judges, kings and prophets. It allots to Israel a territory, and for a national program assigns the conquest of that land (as previously noted) with a view to the establishment there of Yahweh's cult and rule. It deals with offenses of the whole community (see, e.g., Lev. 4:13) and imposes sanctions which are matters of national weal and woe.[13] Its negative aspect expressed in prohibition and excommunication serves a corporate function, fashioning by its exclusive limits the shape of the community.[14] This community-structuring or constitutional character of Old Testament law in general, which shows it to be plainly an extension of the stipulations section of the foundational treaties, will be found to have special importance when it comes to the question of the essential function of biblical canon.

There are also certain stylistic features of Old Testament laws that help to identify them as treaty stipulations. Among these is the combination of case laws with apodictic laws in the form of direct address.[15] Another is

[13] The presence of national penalties to be executed by God alongside penalties to be imposed by human authorities further distinguishes Pentateuchal law from the extrabiblical law collections.

[14] Cf. von Rad, *Old Testament Theology* (tr. D. M. G. Stalker; New York, 1965), II, 391f. See also the next note.

[15] Cf. S. M. Paul, *Studies in the Book of the Covenant in the Light of Cuneiform and Biblical Law* (Leiden, 1970), pp. 118-124.

the hortatory reinforcement of the stipulations,[16] the exhortations tying Israel's obligations in with the history of Yahweh's covenant mercies to the nation.

History

Historical narrative constitutes a major part of the Old Testament canon. A prominent feature of the historical materials in the Pentateuch is that they are interwoven with legislation. This literary combination is a formal indication of the covenantal nature of the Pentateuchal narratives and legislation alike. For this unusual union of history and law was distinctive of the treaties. In the treaties of the second millennium B.C., in particular, an historical prologue was introductory to the section on obligations. Agreeably, in recognized covenantal units in the Pentateuch like the Decalogue and Deuteronomy, the laws are preceded by an historical review of Yahweh's relationship to Israel. If the Pentateuch is viewed as a unified corpus with God's covenant with the exodus generation of Israel as its nucleus, the narratives of Genesis and the first part of Exodus assume the character of an historical prologue tracing that covenantal relationship to its historical roots in Yahweh's past dealings with the chosen people and their patriarchal ancestors.[17]

In addition to serving as a prologue to the treaty law, historical narrative might appear within the treaty stipula-

---

Contrasting apodictic to casuistic laws, he observes that the former have the effect of shaping the community through the absolute ideal they prescribe.

[16] Cf. von Rad, *op. cit.*, I, 196ff.

[17] The function of a treaty preamble is performed by the opening chapters of Genesis, most strikingly by the unusual combination of Yahweh and *'elôhîm* as designations for God in chapters 2 and 3. This opening section of the book identifies the suzerain. It proclaims that Yahweh, covenant Lord of Israel, is the almighty Creator of heaven and earth and all their hosts. In making these observations, our contention is not, of course, that the Pentateuch as such is a treaty in form.

tions as a special setting for a particular obligation, indicating the circumstances out of which it arose. Thus, in the midst of the stipulations of the treaty of Tudhaliyas IV and Ulmi-Teshub the suzerain inserts an account of how the provision concerning the vassal's military support had originated.[18] It is related that in preparing a supplementary treaty tablet on this subject on an earlier occasion the suzerain had observed that the vassal nation's previous obligation had been excessive and he had accordingly modified it. The revised form of the stipulation on the tablet prepared on that occasion was prefaced by this historical explanation so that that tablet as well as the text of the present treaty with Ulmi-Teshub contained the feature of history used as a framework for a particular law. So, too, in the Pentateuch, historical narrative serves as a special setting for individual covenantal stipulations.[19]

The post-Pentateuchal historical narratives no longer perform the same formal literary role as prologue and framework for treaty laws. Thematically, however, they are seen to be nothing other than an extension of the historical prologues of the foundational Mosaic treaties in the Pentateuch. For their theme is first and last Yahweh's relationship to Israel as their covenant Lord.[20] The nar-

[18] Cf. McCarthy, *op. cit.*, pp. 183f., for a translation of this treaty.

[19] See, e.g., passages like Numbers 27:1ff. and 36:1ff. Compare the interweaving of history and related cultic stipulations in Exodus 12.

[20] On the basis of links between Assyrian annals and letters to the gods, plus the testimony of art, the Assyrian historiography may be interpreted as having been originally designed to magnify the gods. The gods' guidance by means of omens and their valorous involvement in military campaigns were the ultimate explanation of success. Entailed in this was a broadly theocratic view of national history, which comes to expression in the interpretation of calamities as retribution for offenses against the gods. An example of such offense is the violation of international treaties sworn by the gods, and in such a case the retribution might be

ratives rehearse the continuing benefits bestowed by Yahweh as faithful Protector of his vassal kingdom. They tell how he graciously intervened for their preservation and enrichment, championing their cause in conflict, even as of old he brought them out of the iron furnace of Egypt to the covenantal communion table at Sinai. They relate how he staffed their ranks with judges and kings, priests and prophets, for the development of the kingdom after the pattern that had been prescribed in the constitutional stipulations of the Pentateuch. At the same time Old Testament historiography pursues the countertheme of Israel's repeated covenant-breaking and the consequent infliction on them of the evils delineated beforehand in the curse sanctions of the Mosaic treaties, particularly in Deuteronomy.[21]

Indeed, the covenantal orientation controls the entire disposition of these narratives, the arrangement as well as the selection of the materials. Thus, episodes of covenant-making and of covenant reaffirmation and renewal after Israel's lapse and Yahweh's judgments provide the climactic literary high points (see, e.g., Josh. 8:30ff.; 23 and 24; 1 Sam. 12; 2 Sam. 7; 2 Kings 11:17ff.; 22 and 23; 2 Chron. 15:8ff.; 34 and 35; Ezra 9 and 10; Neh. 9 and 10).[22]

There is a virtual acknowledgment of this essentially covenantal nature of Old Testament historiography in the

---

described in the annals in the language of treaty curses. See E. A. Speiser's treatment of Mesopotamia in *The Idea of History in the Ancient Near East* (ed. R. C. Dentan; New Haven, 1955), pp. 64ff.

[21] Noth observes that the narrative tradition of the history of Israel was preserved along with the law "as a collection of historical examples of the attitude of man to the law and its consequences" (*op. cit.*, p. 87).

[22] See Baltzer, *op. cit.*, pp. 48-87. It has also been observed that the narratives in Deuteronomy-2 Kings are marked by a series of interpretive speeches and essays in a pattern of covenantal program and fulfillment. Cf. D. J. McCarthy, *Kings and Prophets* (Milwaukee, 1968).

currently popular higher critical theory that the material in Joshua through 2 Kings was shaped by an alleged Deuteronomistic school. On this approach, the Book of Deuteronomy is thought to have been produced as a programmatic introduction for the following history work, the latter being then understood as an interpretation of the life of Israel in terms of the theology of history expressed in Deuteronomy. Though unacceptable as an account of the origin of the literature in question,[23] this view is not mistaken when it finds the distinctive trait of these narratives to be their historical demonstration of the theological principles spelled out in the Book of Deuteronomy. And that is in effect to say that this historical treatment is covenantal, for Deuteronomy is precisely the treaty document given by Yahweh through Moses to be the canonical foundation of Israel's life in covenant relationship to himself. It may be added that modern higher critical studies of Chronicles, Ezra, and Nehemiah point to their covenantal orientation too. They are often seen as the product of the "Chronicler"; but whatever their origins, the selection of data for narration reveals their primary and pervasive interest in the cultic and dynastic institutions by which the covenant relationship of Yahweh with Israel was maintained.

While the history beyond the Pentateuch is thus to be identified as an extension of the historical prologues of the Mosaic treaties, its close connection with the prophets and the prophetic literature of the Old Testament is also to be noted. This interrelationship is another mark of the covenantal nature of the history, for the prophets pursued a distinctly covenantal vocation.

The Chronicler's references to historical sources composed by prophets (see 1 Chron. 29:29; 2 Chron. 9:29; 12:15; 13:22; 20:34; 26:22; 32:32; 33:19; cf. also Isa. 36-39) and the tradition of the prophetic authorship of the history of post-Mosaic times in Joshua through 2

[23] Cf. *TGK*, pp. 30ff.

Kings[24] attest to the activity of prophets in recording the history of Yahweh's covenant people. The missions of various prophets are related in these narratives, certain of them being prominently featured. Also, it has often been observed that the Old Testament historical narratives are complementary to the prophetic writings known as the Latter Prophets, providing the necessary framework to understand them. The design of the history, however, went beyond the merely literary function of providing a background for the interpretation of the prophetic messages. The historical documents were suitable for legal service in the administration of the covenant. They constituted the official record witnessing to Yahweh's fidelity and to the vassal people's continual noncompliance with his commandments. In them the prophets had in hand documentary testimony substantiating their case in their mission as agents of Yahweh's covenant lawsuit against Israel.[25]

In brief, we have now seen that Old Testament historical records, Pentateuchal and post-Pentateuchal, are extensions of the treaty prologues. They stand linked to both law and prophecy, and on both scores served as an instrument of covenant administration.

Prophecy

The question of the covenantal nature of the Latter Prophets may be approached through the office of their authors. Those who fulfilled the prophetic office were Yahweh's messengers, not only in the general sense that they were inspired agents of revelation (though they, along with others, were of course that), but in the particular sense that they performed a distinctive diplomatic function.

The label "prophet" was employed in a more general

---

24 Hence these books are called the Former Prophets.

25 See further below.

sense, and the entire Old Testament revelation might be viewed as a revelation through God's prophets (cf. Heb. 1:1). It is, however, methodologically unsound to appeal to this broader, charismatic usage to obscure the difference between the revelatory gift and the administrative office and so to deny the existence of the prophetic office.[26] Adequate procedure requires that word study be conjoined with sociological analysis, and such analysis plainly discloses the presence of a specific prophetic function and office in Israel. The prophets were the representatives of Yahweh in the administration of his covenant over Israel to declare his claims and enforce his will through effective proclamation.[27]

The establishment of the prophetic office was itself a matter of treaty stipulation. Moses, prophet-mediator of the old covenant, arranged in the Deuteronomic treaty for his covenantal task to be furthered by a succession of prophets like unto himself (Deut. 18:15ff.; cf. Exod. 4:16; 7:1f.).[28]

The peculiarly prophetic task was the elaboration and application of the ancient covenant sanctions. In actual

[26] Thus R. L. Harris, "Factors Promoting the Formation of the OT Canon," *Bulletin of the Evangelical Theological Society*, X, 1 (1967), 21ff.

[27] In his study, *Prophecy and Covenant* (Naperville, 1965), R. E. Clements states that "the distinctiveness of the canonical prophets . . . lay in their particular relationship to, and concern with, the covenant between Yahweh and Israel" (p. 127) as they "actualized the covenant tradition in a situation of crisis, in which the old order had fallen into decay" (p. 123). He presents this thesis in connection with the more general acknowledgment that "the controlling factor" in the development of the several literary traditions in the Old Testament was Israel's knowledge of covenant relationship to Yahweh (pp. 23f.).

[28] Muilenburg concludes that the prophets were "like Moses, Yahweh's messengers, his covenant mediators . . . sent from the divine King, the suzerain of the treaties." See his "The 'Office' of the Prophet in Ancient Israel," in *The Bible in Modern Scholarship* (ed. J. P. Hyatt; Nashville, 1965), p. 97.

practice this meant that their diplomatic mission to Israel was by and large one of prosecuting Yahweh's patient covenant lawsuit with his incurably wayward vassal people.[29] The documentary legacy of their mission reveals them confronting Israel with judgment. These writings mirror the several sections of the original treaty pattern—preamble, historical prologue, stipulations, and sanctions—in new configurations suitable to the prophets' distinctive function. They proclaim the sovereign name of the covenant Lord: Yahweh, Creator, God of hosts. They rehearse the gracious acts of his reign through the history of his relationship with Israel.[30] They reiterate interpretively the obligations his treaty has imposed (cf. Ezra 9:11; Dan. 9:10), calling into review Israel's rebellious ways, and they confront the sinful nation with the curses threatened in treaty text and ratificatory rite, while renewing promises of unquenchable grace. Manifestly, then, these writings of the prophets are extensions of the covenantal documents of Moses. They summon Israel to remember the law covenant of Moses commanded at Horeb (Mal. 4:4) and to behold the eschatological future whose outlines were already sketched in the Mosaic curse and blessing sanctions, particularly in the covenant renewal in Moab (Deut. 28ff.).[31]

The covenantal nature of the prophets' office and message is reflected in various details of the language and form of their writings. The evidence for this is not only inner-biblical. Along with the links between the prophets and the specifically Mosaic covenants, parallels can be traced between the prophetic literature and the documents of international covenant diplomacy.

Numerous studies have demonstrated how the prophets' use of various key words follows the usage in the

[29] Cf. *BOC*, pp. 51ff.

[30] See also what was said above about the role of the prophets in recording the history of the covenant relationship.

[31] Cf. *TGK*, pp. 34, 124ff., and 132f.

extrabiblical covenant literature.[32] Beyond individual lexical items there are broader matters of form, most important among these the much discussed covenant lawsuit genre. The formulary for the prosecution of treaty violators can be reconstructed, largely from ancient royal letters, and it has been found that the prophetic indictment of Israel repeatedly follows this pattern of the covenant lawsuit.[33] One frequently noted element in this form is the prophets' appeal to heaven and earth to serve as witnesses.[34] Another important area of correspondence with the treaties, both biblical and extrabiblical, is the prophets' threats of judgment. Many close parallels have been pointed out between the specific kinds of evil threatened by the prophets, including the accompanying terminology and imagery, and the curses in the sanctions section of the treaties.[35] It has also been suggested that

[32] Illustrating by the prophets' use of the word "know" in the technical meanings which it has in the international treaties, Hillers observes that though "the word 'covenant' is not prominently on display in their writings, the complex of ideas associated with covenant is present as an invisible framework" (*Covenant*, pp. 123f.). Cf. J. Limburg, "The Root *[rîb]* and the Prophetic Lawsuit Speeches," *Journal of Biblical Literature*, LXXXVIII, 3 (1969), 291ff., esp. pp. 303f.

[33] Cf. *TGK*, p. 35, n. 26, and p. 139. See above, n. 6. Cf. also J. Harvey, *Le plaidoyer prophétique contre Israël après la rupture de l'alliance* (Paris, 1967); R. North, "Angel-Prophet or Satan-Prophet?", *Zeitschrift für die alttestamentliche Wissenschaft*, LXXXII (1970), 31ff., esp. pp. 64ff.; M. O'Rourke Boyle, "The Covenant Lawsuit of the Prophet Amos: III 1—IV 13," *Vetus Testamentum*, XXI, 3 (1971), 338-362.

[34] On this see J. R. Boston, "The Wisdom Influence upon the Song of Moses," *Journal of Biblical Literature*, LXXXVII, 2 (1968), 198f.; and North, *op. cit.*, pp. 48f., 52, 58.

[35] See especially Hillers, *Treaty-Curses and the Old Testament Prophets* and *Covenant*, pp. 131ff. The parallels occur frequently in prophetic oracles on foreign nations. The meaning of that must be related to the fundamental fact that the blessing of God's people has as its corollary the subjugation of their enemies. It is not just that Israel's curses and blessings are mirror-images of each

the summons to repentance is a distinct prophetic speech-type and that it reflects treaty formulations. Specifically, the peculiar structure of the summons, consisting of admonition-promise-accusation-threat, is traced to a double set of covenantal protasis and apodosis conditions.[36]

It would appear that the covenant emissaries sent by the great kings to deal with their vassals provided a model for the office of the biblical prophets sent by the Lord to his covenant servants. This is supported by data such as we have surveyed showing that the message of the prophets was in significant respects cast in the traditional categories and conventional language of international treaty administration. This interpretation of the situation is strengthened further by the discovery of an interesting historical coincidence in the area of diplomatic technique.[37]

It has been observed that in the development of Assyrian statecraft a shift took place in connection with late ninth- and early eighth-century imperial expansion. Hitherto, the ambassadorial messenger of the Assyrian suzerain had addressed himself to the vassal king and his court, but now such missions began to be directed to the vassal populace as well. Within the history of Israel a similar development occurred at the same time. In the

other (as often in the treaties), but that whichever Israel receives, her foes receive the other. If one is head, the other is tail (cf. Deut. 28:7, 13, 25). For in establishing the Abrahamic community as his protectorate, God promised to curse those who cursed his people (Gen. 12:3). On the usage of these oracles within the institutional life of Israel see the analysis of J. H. Hayes, "The Usage of Oracles Against Foreign Nations in Ancient Israel," *Journal of Biblical Literature*, LXXXVII, 1 (1968), 81-92.

[36] Thus T. M. Raitt, "The Prophetic Summons to Repentance," *Zeitschrift für die alttestamentliche Wissenschaft*, LXXXIII (1971), 30-49.

[37] For this see J. S. Holladay, Jr., "Assyrian Statecraft and the Prophets of Israel," *Harvard Theological Review*, LXIII (1970), 29-51.

first two centuries of the monarchy the mission of the prophets had been closely identified with the royal court,[38] but with the emergence of the writing prophets in the eighth century the covenant people as a whole became the objects of the address of Yahweh's messengers.

While relating the prophetic office to covenants in general, all such literary and technical parallels pointing to the political sphere of suzerain-vassal relationship as the formal background for the prophetic office serve also as another link, even if indirect, connecting the prophets with the covenants of Moses, inasmuch as the form of the latter, too, derives from that very same background of covenantal statecraft.

Praise

What the relationship of the Psalter was to the cult has been the subject of much discussion. Whatever may be concluded about the cultic origins of the various *Gattungen* represented in the Psalter or of the individual psalms themselves, certainly many psalms were employed in Israel's cult, even if the definition of cult were to be restricted to the service of worship in the immediate charge of the Levitical ministry. And since the temple was the sacramental focal point of the prayers of Israel from locales domestic and foreign (cf. 1 Kings 8:29ff.), it may be said that the psalms in general are cultically oriented. This means that the covenant is the Psalter's sphere of existence.[39]

[38] Cf. G. Vos, *Biblical Theology* (Grand Rapids, 1948), pp. 204ff.

[39] See the remarks above on cult, and notice further how the temple dedication prayer of Solomon, which gives classic expression to the practice of directing prayer toward the Jerusalem temple, is concerned from first to last with the covenant situation, its promises and its curse sanctions.

The psalms of praise, whether magnifying the majesty of Yahweh's person or the wonder of his ways in creation or redemption, were a part of Israel's tributary obligations; they were the spiritual sacrifices of the lips offered to the Great King. As vehicles of private and public devotion they were a continual resounding of Israel's "Amen" of covenant ratification. Psalms that rehearsed the course of covenant history (see, e.g., Pss. 78, 105-106, 135-136) were confessional responses of acknowledgment to the surveys of Yahweh's mighty acts in Israel's behalf which were contained in the historical prologues of the treaties, responses suitable for recitation in ceremonies of covenant reaffirmation where those acts were memorialized (cf. Deut. 26:1ff.; Josh. 24:16-18). In the use of the psalms extolling the law of God, Israel submitted anew to the stipulations of the covenant. Plaint and penitential psalms might find a place in interaction with the prophetic indictment of Israel in the process of the covenant lawsuit.[40] Thus, the case for the covenantal function of the Psalter does not depend on a theory (like Weiser's) that would assign much in the Psalter a role in some one annual covenant renewal festival, speculatively reconstructed. Rather, the Psalter served broadly as a cultic instrument in the maintenance of a proper covenantal relationship with Yahweh.

The Psalter's function in covenantal confession suggests that it may be regarded as an extension of the vassal's ratification response, which is found in certain biblical as well as extrabiblical covenants as part of the treaty text.[41] There are other aspects to the literary relations of the Psalter to the treaty form. Muilenburg

[40] J. Harvey, *op. cit.*, pp. 157-163, concludes that the covenant lawsuit issued in an acknowledgment by the party judged. In the Old Testament this is found in confessional prayers of the *tôdâ* genre. Harvey finds the association of covenant lawsuit and *tôdâ* clearly attested in Psalm 50.

[41] Cf. *TGK*, p. 29, and see further below.

remarks on "the degree to which the covenant terminology and form were adopted for use in worship" in
Israel, noting psalms like 50, 81, 89, and 132 and extra-
Psalter prayers like Solomon's at the dedication of the
temple.[42] Analysis of the structure of various types of
psalms may be fruitfully pursued by comparison with the
thematic sequence of the treaties. Baltzer traces the influence of the covenant form in the liturgy of later Judaism,
including Qumran texts, and early Christianity.[43] How
completely appropriate, then, that the Psalter opens with
an echo of the treaty blessings and curses and the declaration that judgment hinges on man's attitude towards the
law of the covenant.[44]

Wisdom

The central thesis of the wisdom books is that wisdom
begins with the fear of Yahweh, which is to say that the
way of wisdom is the way of the covenant. In the
Deuteronomic treaty Moses affirms that Israel received
wisdom as an objective gift from Yahweh when he set
before the nation the righteous statutes of his covenant
and that Israel's subjective possession of wisdom was to
be made manifest in their keeping the covenant (Deut.
4:6-8; cf. Jer. 8:8; Ezra 7:14, 25).[45]

Accordingly, the function of the wisdom literature of

[42] See his "The Form and Structure of the Covenant Formula-
tion," in *Vetus Testamentum,* IX (1959), 356, with nn. 2 and 3. Cf.
J. H. Tigay, "Psalm 7:5 and Ancient Near Eastern Treaties,"
Journal of Biblical Literature, LXXXIX (1970), 178-186; and A.
R. Millard, "For He Is Good," *Tyndale Bulletin,* XVII (1966),
115-117.

[43] *Op. cit.,* pp. 171ff.

[44] Psalm 1 uses the terms "walk" and "know" in their technical
treaty sense. Notice, too, the mirror-image relation of the similes
employed in this psalm to depict the dual sanctions.

[45] Cf. G. E. Wright, *The Old Testament and Theology* (New
York, 1969), p. 76, n. 8.

the Old Testament is the explication of the covenant. One way it performs this is by translating the covenant stipulations into maxims and instructions regulative of conduct in the different areas of life and under its varying conditions. But the wisdom books are equally concerned with the outworking of the covenant sanctions in human experience. This association of wisdom with the revelation of the covenantal sanctions is already prominent in the Mosaic treaties. The Song of Witness in Deuteronomy 32:1-43 is a remarkably complete formulation of the covenant lawsuit, prophetically promulgated at the ratification of the Deuteronomic treaty. It anticipates Israel's subsequent rebelliousness and announces beforehand how Yahweh, stirred to jealousy, would heap upon them the evils so fully portrayed in the sanctions section of the treaty. And Moses introduces this Song as his "teaching," so identifying it by terminology common for instruction in the wisdom literature.[46]

Thus to the knowledge of what God requires, Old Testament wisdom is concerned to add understanding of how God deals with individuals,[47] sovereignly meting out prosperity and adversity in his government of a fallen world in process of redemption. Or better, Old Testament wisdom sets forth the general order of divine providence and gives instruction as to the life stance appropriate to Yahweh's servants living within that world order regulated by his covenants. The exposition of this topic inevitably leads to a pondering of the mystery of the sufferings of God's servants. In the present connection it

[46] Cf. *TGK*, p. 139. The extensive use of wisdom motifs in the Song is traced by Boston (*op. cit.*). On Deuteronomy and wisdom literature, cf. J. Malfroy, "Sagesse et loi dans le Deuteronomie," *Vetus Testamentum*, XV (1965), 49ff.

[47] It is characteristic of the wisdom books that they analyze the situation of the individual rather than the corporate community and that their scope extends beyond the individual covenant servant within the context of the peculiar sanction guarantees given to the theocratic nation Israel.

need only be noted that it is the Old Testament wisdom literature's function of interpreting the sanctions of Yahweh's covenants that explains the intensity of its involvement with the question of theodicy.

There are close links between the wisdom books and Israel's covenantal institutions, royal, prophetic, and cultic.[48] Not a little of the canonical wisdom is attributable to King Solomon, who also figures as royal patron of the wisdom enterprise in general. The interrelationship of the wisdom and prophetic movements is observable in shared literary themes and techniques. We have seen above that the covenant lawsuit, the prosecution of which looms so large in the prophetic mission, is cast in the form of wisdom instruction in Deuteronomy 32. The allied theme of theodicy,[49] prominently treated in the wisdom literature, is also a prophetic theme. Thus, Lamentations might be regarded as a prophetic wisdom book; it applies the wisdom motif of theodicy to the peculiarly prophetic province of the corporate history of Israel under the Mosaic covenant.

An important point of contact between Old Testament wisdom and the treaties, biblical and extrabiblical, is their common concern that their precepts be transmitted to successive generations through parental instruction of children. The parallel is strikingly reinforced by the coupling of this theme with the insistence that obedience be rendered with the whole heart and also with the provision that obedience be prompted by binding the precepts to the body as signs. For examples of this interesting complex of ideas see, on the wisdom side, Proverbs 3:1ff.; 6:20f.; and 7:1ff. and, on the treaty side,

[48] D. A. Hubbard surveys these matters in "The Wisdom Movement and Israel's Covenant Faith," *Tyndale Bulletin*, XVII (1966), 3-33, esp. pp. 7-15.

[49] The condemnation of the vassal is in view in the lawsuit, while the justification of Yahweh is the aim in theodicy; but lawsuit has theodicy as its corollary.

Deuteronomy 4 (a passage which closely combines the treaty document clause and an identification of the covenant way with wisdom, vv. 2-8); 6:1ff.; and 11:13ff. (see also Jer. 31:31ff.; cf. Prov. 3:3; 7:3).[50] The appearance of Yahweh's covenantal words in the wisdom form of parental instruction reminds us that the covenantal and family models offer complementary understandings of God's relationship to man. The Lord of the covenant is also the Father of his people (see Deut. 1:31; 8:5; 14:1; 32:5ff.; 1 Cor. 8:5f.).[51]

Summary

From the foregoing sampling of the data it can be seen that the foundational treaty form which was adopted in the Mosaic covenants anticipated in its composite pattern the subsequent development of the Old Testament.[52] The treaty form was a remarkable documentary epitome of the whole covenant relationship. In it we see a corolla of petals tightly compacted, while in the Old Testament canon as a whole we see this covenant corolla unfolded in

[50] For these features in the extrabiblical covenants see, for example, Esarhaddon's Nimrud treaty (lines 283ff. and 385ff.). Cf., too, my "Abram's Amen," *Westminster Theological Journal*, XXXI, 1 (1968), 11, and n. 26.

[51] Cf. D. J. McCarthy, "Notes on the Love of God in Deuteronomy and the Father-Son Relationship between Yahweh and Israel," *Catholic Biblical Quarterly*, XXVII, 2 (1965), 144-147; and M. Weinfeld, "The Covenant of Grant in the Old Testament and in the Ancient Near East," *Journal of the American Oriental Society*, XC, 2 (1970), 194.

[52] This is not, of course, to claim that all the literary variegation disclosed by form-critical analysis of the Old Testament was present in the treaty form, nor even that particular features common to, say, the prophetic or wisdom books and the treaties were peculiar to the treaties in extrabiblical literature or even had their ultimate source in them. The relationships of the various forms, even in their employment within the Old Testament limits, were intricately interdependent.

flower. In this process of organic extension there was combined with the Pentateuchal record of the establishment of the covenant a centuries-spanning documentary witness to the continuing relationship, consisting in historical accounts, documents of the prophetic emissaries of the Lord, and literary deposits of other aspects of covenant life. The Old Testament which was thus produced represents an adaptation of the treaty form which is as much creative as it is imitative. Hence, the Old Testament is a covenantal corpus which is not only materially but formally *sui generis*. But it is indeed as a whole a *covenantal* corpus.

Covenantal New Testament

For the sake of obtaining a total biblical picture something must be said about the identity of the New Testament, too, as a covenantal corpus. Here, however, we must be content with little more than a bare statement of our thesis, looking hopefully to colleagues whose specialization is in this area to develop the matter in detail.

The identity of the various parts of the New Testament as in a distinct, functional-literary sense covenantal will be more readily discerned if we have first arrived at a covenantal assessment of the New Testament as a whole. And the latter follows quite clearly once our conclusions concerning the covenantal nature of the Old Testament are accepted. For the historical relationship sustained by the new covenant to the old covenant and the place occupied by the New Testament as the divine documentation of the new covenant compel us to understand the New Testament as a resumption of that documentary mode of covenant administration represented by the Old Testament.

The New Testament belongs to that pattern of renewing covenants by the issuance of new treaty documents which is already found in the inner history of old

covenant administration.[53] Thus, for example, the Deuteronomic treaty documented the renewal of the covenant contained in the Sinaitic tables. This feature of the
process of covenant administration constitutes another of
the many parallels between biblical and extrabiblical
covenants. In the case of the latter, not only might changing circumstances result in the altering of treaty provisions (as illustrated in the example dealing with military
provisions noted above), but total renewals of the covenant relationship took place, especially on the occasion
of changing leadership, whether on the suzerain or vassal
side. And these changes and renewals were witnessed to
by the preparation of new treaty documents.[54]

It is apparent how suitable a model for the Scriptural
revelation was supplied by such a series of treaties docu-
menting the continuing renewal of a covenant relationship. For the redemptive history with which the Scriptures were organically connected proceeded by means of
a succession of renewals of God's covenantal relationship
to his people. The dynamics of eschatological progress in
this renewal movement of redemptive history are unique.
Nevertheless, the comprehensive schema of this history as
it is reflected in the Scriptures' major division into old,
pre-Messianic and new, Messianic testaments clearly re-
produces the formal ancient pattern of treaty-documented covenant renewal. The covenant model with its

[53] The consummatory nature of *the* new covenant must be
recognized, but the point made above remains valid. Cf. *BOC*, pp.
75f. and n. 26.

[54] See Baltzer's analysis of the occasions of covenant reaffirmation and renewal in the Old Testament (*op. cit.*, pp. 59ff., 71ff.).
In the historical prologues of the Hittite treaties references are
found to previous treaty transactions with the vassal or his predecessors, occasions being mentioned when renewal of the covenant had been called for by circumstances like change in the
dynastic succession or restoration of the vassal after violation of
the treaty. Cf. *TGK*, pp. 36ff.; and J. Harvey, *op. cit.*, pp. 55,
131ff.

mode of administrative continuity thus accounts for the overall structure of Scripture as Old and New Testaments, and hence it also accounts in particular for the New Testament as a whole, standing in literary relationship to the Old Testament.[55]

When we come to the New Testament, it may be questioned whether the human authors were still conscious of the international treaty model lying behind biblical covenant and canon. Diplomatic traditions would exhibit a measure of continuity in treaty praxis through the centuries, and some of the New Testament writers possibly had more awareness of the ancient extrabiblical covenants than one might guess. But in any case these writers were well acquainted with the secular treaty structure in its embodiment in the Old Testament. However ignorant they were of the formal origins of the covenantal structure, they were fully familiar with the treaty form itself as they found it in their Scriptures. They realized, too, that the covenant that was being documented in their own writings was the renewal and fulfillment of the old covenant documented in the Old Testament Scriptures. By taking a place as authors in that succession they were in fact, if not consciously, adopting the model of the ancient state treaty traditions, including in particular the techniques of covenant renewal.[56] And our point is that in the international covenants the providential ordering of the God of the Bible had made

[55] At the same time, this case for the covenantal understanding of the relation of the two Testaments in the overall structure of Scripture supports the position affirmed above concerning the covenantal identification of the Old Testament as a whole and in its several major divisions.

[56] There were human authors of the Bible who, when portraying the new covenant in relation to the old, were conscious of the structural parallels to this relationship in political treaty administration. For Old Testament authors like Moses and Jeremiah wrote prophetically of the new covenant as the Messianic restoration of the covenant broken by Israel (e.g., Deut. 30:1-10; Jer. 31:31-34).

available a model most serviceable for the documentary expression of biblical religion.

In the case of the New Testament as in that of the Old Testament, acceptance of its own claims as to its primary divine authorship leads to recognition of its pervasively covenantal nature and purpose. For the New Testament so received will be understood as the word of the ascended Lord of the new covenant, by which he structures the community of the new covenant and orders the faith and life of his servant people in their consecrated relationship to him. And then the human authors of the New Testament books, authorized by their Lord to speak his word, will be seen to function as his "ministers of the new covenant" (cf. 2 Cor. 3:6). With respect to immediate as well as ultimate provenance, the *Sitz im Leben* of the New Testament books is fundamentally covenantal. They all arise out of a covenantal source of authority and all address themselves to the covenant community.

The several literary genres represented by the individual books of the New Testament are not the same as the major Old Testament genres. But, as in the case of the latter, their covenantal functions can be readily related to particular sections of the foundational treaty form. Each one is rather transparently a specialized adaptation of one petal or another of the treaty corolla. Once again, therefore, there is a literary as well as functional aspect to the covenantal identification of these biblical books.

Though it would be the task of New Testament canonics to elaborate this thesis, the main outlines are obvious enough at once. From the gospels and Acts the lines can be traced back through the Old Testament historical narratives to the Pentateuchal records of the founding of the old covenant, with the Genesis prologue thereto, and thus back to the historical prologue section of the Mosaic treaties. The gospels and Acts also perform the function of the treaty preambles by introducing the Messianic Lord of the covenant and identifying him through various witnesses as the divine King of Israel, son of David, and eternal Word.

Like the covenant narrative in the Pentateuch, that in the gospels is chiefly concerned with the establishment of the covenant order. It is particularly in their dominant interest in the sacrificial death of Christ, the covenant mediator, that the gospels show themselves to be primarily testimonies to the ratification of God's covenant.[57] What precedes the passion narratives in the gospels serves a prologue function (like that of the Book of Genesis in connection with the Sinaitic covenant), relating the background of previous covenant history. What follows the gospel records of the ratification of the new covenant, that is, the history in the Book of Acts,[58] corresponds to the post-Sinai narratives of the Old Testament as an account of the effective founding of the covenant community in its historical role and mission.[59] In providing an historical framework for the epistolary portion of the New Testament canon, the Book of Acts functions in a manner similar to the Former Prophets in relation to the Latter Prophets in the Old Testament.

From the New Testament epistles the lines can be traced back primarily through the prophets, but also through the Old Testament books of wisdom and worship, to the law of the Mosaic treaties, both stipulations and sanctions, particularly to the element of parenesis there. The kind of structural parallelism with the treaties that Baltzer notes in early Christian literature like the

[57] As frequently observed, the gospels are not strictly biographies of Jesus. The interpretation of the gospel form as covenant ratification witness or, more generally, as covenant record should provide a helpful clue in dealing with questions of the selection and disposition of the gospel materials, matters which a biographical approach would often leave problematic.

[58] The Luke-Acts unity indicates that the primary character of the gospels as covenantal records must apply to Acts too.

[59] Some further analysis of this will be necessary under a subsequent discussion of canonical norms.

Epistle of Barnabas, the Didache, and 2 Clement[60] is also present in the New Testament epistles. One aspect of the covenantal mission of Israel's prophets which finds an illuminating counterpart in the letters of the apostle Paul is that of the prosecution of Yahweh's covenant lawsuit. Although this is not as prominent in the first generation mission of the apostolic minister of the new covenant, arresting evidence of such a function is found in a recurring motif in Paul's letters that has been called "the apostolic parousia."[61] The epistle itself was an anticipatory surrogate for the apostle's presence in disciplinary power.[62] It was also by means of letters, as noted above, that ancient suzerains conducted their covenant lawsuits. The judgment section of Paul's letters, in particular, have been found to exhibit a purpose and pattern (introduction-offense-punishment-hortatory conclusion) in imitation of the prophetic judgments on Israel.[63]

Once again from the New Testament Apocalypse the lines can be traced through the Old Testament prophets

[60] *Op. cit.*, pp. 128ff.

[61] See R. W. Funk, "The Apostolic 'Parousia': Form and Significance," in *Christian History and Interpretation* (ed. W. R. Farmer, C. F. D. Moule, R. R. Niebuhr; Cambridge, 1967), pp. 249-268. Cf. A. R. Millard, "Covenant and Communion in First Corinthians," in *Apostolic History and the Gospel* (ed. W. W. Gasque and R. P. Martin; Grand Rapids, 1970), pp. 242-248, esp. p. 247. He sees ancient covenantal features in several other New Testament elements, especially in various aspects of the Lord's Supper. Of special interest in connection with our study of canonical sanctions protecting treaty texts (see Ch. 1 above) is the parallel Millard finds in the ideas that the new covenant is written on the hearts of the vassals and that those who violate such vassals, leading them into apostasy, are cursed.

[62] Another aspect of the apostolic parousia short of the apostle's personal presence was the representative apostolic emissary.

[63] So C. Roetzel, "The Judgment Form in Paul's Letters," *Journal of Biblical Literature*, LXXXVIII (1969), 305-312. Cf. J. L. White, "Introductory Formulae in the Body of the Pauline Letter," *Journal of Biblical Literature*, XC (1971), 91-97.

to the eschatological curses and blessings of the sanctions section of the treaties. The Book of Revelation is replete with treaty analogues from its opening preamble-like identification of the awesome Lord Christ; through the letters to the churches, administering Christ's covenantal lordship after the manner of the ancient lawsuit; on through the elaborately expounded prophetic sanctions which constitute the major part of the book; and down to the closing documentary clause and canonical curse.

As was the case in the Old Testament, the New Testament's adaptation of the treaty structure is highly creative. Being far less directly related than was the Old Testament to that world of ancient diplomacy, the New Testament writings reflect here and there rather than reproduce en bloc its peculiar literary formularies. They were shaped by the special historical circumstances of their own origins and by the literary conventions of their own day. Nevertheless, because of the fundamentally covenantal identity of the New Testament, it, like the Old Testament, was bound to consist of gospel and law— the gospel witnessing to God's establishment of the covenant with his people by historic intervention in sovereign grace, and the law stipulating the community order and mission by which God's people were to fulfill their covenantal service in hope of the parousia of their Lord in the glory of his kingdom. And, in particular, the precise canonical functions of the several distinct literary sections of the New Testament come to proper focus only when seen within the framework of covenant institutions, administration, and documentation.

Conclusion

Our traditional designations "Old Testament" and "New Testament" have been all the while more precisely appropriate than we have realized. According to the common understanding this nomenclature merely reflects the close association of the biblical books with the history of the covenants, or it provides a very succinct table of contents of the Bible. But "testament," or "covenant," denotes more than a prominent element in the contents of the Bible. The documents which combine to form the Bible are in their very nature—a legal sort of nature, it turns out—covenantal. In short, the Bible *is* the old and the new covenants.

We are now in a position to apply what we have earlier concluded concerning biblical canonicity in its treaty origins to the whole of the Old Testament and, indeed, to the entire Scriptures. Because the Bible *is* the old and new covenants and because canon is inherent in covenant of the biblical type, canonicity is inherent in the very form and identity of Scripture as the Old Testament and the New Testament. The canonical authority of the Bible is in a class by itself because its covenantal words are the words of God. Yet because Scripture is covenant, biblical canonicity, from beginning to end, belongs at the formal literary level to the more broadly attested category of authoritative treaty words. All Scripture is covenantal, and the canonicity of all the Scripture is covenantal. [64] Biblical canon is covenantal canon.

[64] Was it out of an awareness of this that *endiathēkos*, "covenantal," was used in the early church instead of *kanōn* to express the canonical character of Scripture? Cf. the usage of Origen and Eusebius in the latter's *Church History*, III, 3, i and iii; III, 25, vi; VI, 25, i.

Chapter Three

CANON AND COVENANT COMMUNITY

Architectural Model for Biblical Canon

Another conceptual model of the Scriptures is suggested by the account of their beginnings found in the Book of Exodus. This other way of viewing the Bible is complementary to the foregoing identification of the Old and New Testaments as the documentary witnesses to the Lord's covenants, old and new. In fact, it brings out more clearly the specific function performed by Scripture in its character as a covenantal document, clarifying in particular the nature of the relationship between biblical canon and covenant community.

The timing of the birth of the Bible was precisely conditioned; there were definite historical prerequisites for its appearance. If the Scriptural form of revelation was to be what it is—God's covenant addressed to the kingdom of his earthly people—then the Bible could have come into existence only when it did. Not earlier, for the appearance of Scripture having the character of kingdom-treaty required as its historical prelude the formation of a community peculiarly God's own and, beyond that, the development of this people to the stage of nationhood under God's lordship.

In the midst of a fallen world and in the face of Satanic hostility manifested in various historical guises, an elect people of God could not attain to kingdom status apart from redemptive judgments delivering them from the power of the adversary. Only when the Lord God had accomplished this soteric triumph would the way be prepared for him to promulgate his kingdom-treaty, setting his commandments among his elect people and ordering their kingdom existence under the dominion of his sovereign will.

In the pre-Messianic age, the Noahic deluge constituted a divine triumph of redemptive judgment by which a remnant community was delivered from the tyranny of the godless and lawless prediluvian world powers[1] and made heirs of a new world. Yet the Noahic community was a family, not a nation to which a kingdom-treaty might appropriately be directed.[2] The necessary conditions were met only in the formation of the nation Israel and only at the Mosaic stage in the course of God's dealings with the Israelite nation. Considerations in addition to the need for a national covenant community made the existence of a special people of revelation a prerequisite for the development of the Scriptures, specifically of the Old Testament. For example, once given the postdiluvian proliferation of nations with their diversity of tongues (Gen. 10 and 11), the elective separation of one people from the diaspora of peoples (Gen. 12ff.) was necessary in order that this one people might serve as the linguistically unified and otherwise cohesive channel re-

[1] Cf. M. G. Kline, "Divine Kingship and Genesis 6:1-4," *Westminster Theological Journal*, XXIV, 2 (1962), 187-204.

[2] Since we are dealing with the theological rationale of the matter, other obviously relevant factors, such as the later origin of writing itself, are omitted above. Theistic discernment will appreciate that the timely invention of writing, too, was embraced in that sovereign providential ordering by which everything was in readiness at the predestined hour for the introduction of Scripture in the historical administration of God's kingdom.

quired for the production of an organically coherent revelation. The redemptive program was not, of course, conceived and executed for the sake of the Scriptures; but the ethno-centralized phase which redemptive history entered when God called Abram out of Ur of the Chaldees is to be accounted for in part by the exigencies of providing the Scriptures as an instrument of salvation.

Covenantal revelation was already addressed to Abraham, Isaac, and Jacob, with their households, offering them the kingdom in promise. But Scripture required for its appearance more than merely the promise of a kingdom. It was necessary that the promise and oath given to the patriarchs be fulfilled; the chosen people must actually attain to nationhood. Not until God had created the kingdom-community of Israel brought forth from Pharaoh's tyranny to the Sinai assembly could he issue canonical covenant of the biblical type. The appearance of canonical Scripture thus had to await the exodus victory of Yahweh. That victory signalized the fulness of time for the birth of God's treaty Word.

The scheduling of the nativity of the written Word at precisely that historical juncture points us to the peculiar quality of canonical Scripture. Originating as it does in consequence of an awesome display of Yahweh's power in salvation and judgment, in accordance with prophetic promises given to the patriarchs, Scripture from the outset bears the character of a word of triumphal fulfillment. It is the incontestable declaration that the name of Israel's God is Yahweh, mighty Lord of the covenant. Although the Mosaic kingdom established at Sinai was itself still only provisional and promissory in relation to the Messianic realities of the New Testament age, yet unmistakably the Old Testament Word of God which heralded the Israelite kingdom was for the pre-Messianic stage of redemptive history a word of promises manifestly fulfilled and of Yahweh's triumphant kingship decisively and dramatically displayed. From its first emergence in the sequel of victory, therefore, canonical Scripture confronts men as a divine word of triumph.

And along with the triumphant there is an architectural aspect to the Bible. For being, as we have seen, a covenantal document, this triumphant Word of God has as its function the structuring of the covenant kingdom. In this connection the imagery of God's "house" comes to the fore in the Book of Exodus. That house is built by means of the canonical Scripture which proceeds from the victorious Yahweh.

In the epic ideology of the ancient Near East it is the god who by virtue of signal victory has demonstrated himself to be king among the gods who then proceeds to build himself a royal residence.[3] A seat of kingship must be established for the exercise of the victorious god's eternal sovereignty. So, for example, in the Canaanite epic of Baal and in the Babylonian *Enuma Elish,* Marduk being the hero-god in the latter, the theme of divine house-building follows that of victory over draconic chaos.

This mythical literary tradition quite clearly lies behind the mode of representation of Israel's redemptive history as recorded in the Book of Exodus. For the same sequence of themes is found again here in Exodus. First, Yahweh judges Egypt and in so doing humbles Egypt's gods (Exod. 12:12; Num. 33:4). To describe these triumphant acts of Yahweh in effecting Israel's escape from servitude under the alien pseudotheocracy, and with particular reference to the passage through the sea, Scripture has recourse to the figure of the slaying of the dragon (Ps. 74:12ff.; Isa. 51:9f.; cf. Ezek. 29:3ff.; 32:2ff.). Then, after his victory over the dragon, Yahweh proceeds to build a house for himself. Such, indeed, is the

[3] Similarly, the legitimation of a king's dynasty is attested by his authorization to build a temple for his god. See A. S. Kapelrud, "Temple Building, A Task for Gods and Kings," *Orientalia,* XXXII, 1 (1963), 56-62.

central theme of all the rest of the Book of Exodus beyond the narrative of the deliverance from Egypt.

Yahweh's house-building, as depicted in Exodus, is of two kinds. There is first the structuring of the people Israel themselves into the formally organized house of Israel. The architectural instrument employed was those constitutional covenant words of God spoken at Sinai which in their documentary form were the beginning of canonical Scripture. Translating into reality the design stipulated in this treaty, the divine Artisan erected the kingdom-house of Israel to be his earthly dwelling place.

Having narrated the building of this living house of God's habitation, the Book of Exodus continues with an account of the building of the other, more literal house of Yahweh, the tabernacle.[4] The erection of this tabernacle-house, too, was arranged through Yahweh's treaty, specifically in the process of elaborating the treaty stipulations. Though a more literal house than the living house of Israel, the tabernacle-house was designed to function as symbolical of the other; the kingdom-people-house was the true residence of God (a concept more fully explored and spiritualized in the New Testament). The Book of Exodus closes by bringing together these two covenant-built houses in a summary statement concerning Yahweh's abiding in glory-cloud in his tabernacle-house "in the sight of all the house of Israel" (40:34-38).

It should be at least parenthetically observed that the literary unity of the Book of Exodus is evidenced by the identification of its comprehensive thematic structure with the pattern of divine triumph and house-building. Classical and still current documentary analysis assigns the extended treatment of the cultic theme of the tabernacle in Exodus 25ff. to the supposed priestly source, while attributing the earlier part of Exodus in the main to

---

[4] From chapter 25 to the end, except for the episode of the breaking and renewal of the covenant in chapters 32-34, the book is devoted to this subject.

the hypothetical narrative sources. This is yet another indication of the unsound methodology of this documentary approach, insufficiently informed by the realities of ancient literature. It arbitrarily puts asunder the sections of Exodus dealing with the themes of divine victory and house-building, which are shown by ancient epics to belong together, and it must then take refuge in the assumption that the authentic ancient pattern in its wholeness emerged quite fortuitously in a late editorial blending of the putative sources into the final form of the book.[5]

Victorious kingship followed by palace-building is discovered as a thematic pattern within the briefer unity of the Song of Triumph at the sea (Exod. 15:1-18), the antiquity of which is generally acknowledged.[6] The Song first celebrates the glorious triumph of redemptive judgment, the demonstration that Yahweh in his majestic holiness and wondrous working was without parallel among the gods (vv. 1-12). Then the Song moves on prophetically to Yahweh's establishment of his sanctuary on the mountain of his abode and the arrival there of his redeemed people through his irresistible might at the site of his everlasting reign (vv. 13-18).

The same perspective on this ancient founding event is

[5] The recognition of the ancient pattern discussed above is a further indication of the fallacy of von Rad's separation of the exodus and Sinai-covenant themes (cf. above, Ch. 1). G. E. Wright plausibly interprets this literary-historical position of von Rad as a reflex of the Lutheran theological separation of law and gospel (*The Old Testament and Theology*, p. 61).

[6] On the classification of this Song in the category of triumphal hymns as attested in the late second millennium B.C., see W. F. Albright, *Yahweh and the Gods of Canaan*, pp. 10f. On the complex of themes in Exodus 15, cf. F. M. Cross, "The Divine Warrior in Israel's Early Cult," in *Biblical Motifs* (ed. A. Altmann; Cambridge, 1966), pp. 22f. and "The Song of the Sea and Canaanite Myth," *Journal for Theology and the Church*, V (1968), 1ff.

echoed back from Psalm 74 with its lament over the contradiction that had come to exist between Yahweh's position as victorious King from of old (vv. 12-17) and the absence of the appropriate residence (vv. 1-11 and 18-23). The literary treatment is in the Exodus tradition. Central once again is the reassertion of God's original supremacy as Creator by his redemptive triumph at the sea, here described as a vanquishing of the dragon, a breaking of Leviathan's heads (13f.). United with the exodus-salvation again is the covenant (20), by which God had constructed for his dwelling both the congregation of his heritage (2) and his sanctuary-house (3ff.). The Psalmist's dismay over the abnormality of the combination of God's indisputably sovereign kingship with the desecrated and desolate state of the dwelling place of his name is a clear reflex of the normal expectation that decisive royal victory would be naturally followed by the building of a permanent royal house.

The pattern that marked the exodus-Sinai foundations of Israel recurs at a later epochal point in the development of the Old Testament kingdom. Yahweh had through his servant David completed the conquest of the enemies round about his earthly domain. Then, fittingly, he arranged by means of the provisions of a covenant for the erection of his temple-house on the holy mount (2 Sam. 7). In this covenant, the dynastic house of David was also established and its permanence guaranteed.

By this configuration of themes Nathan's covenant oracle to David is shown to share with the Song of Exodus 15 in its use of the victory hymn genre. Of incidental but no little interest are literary parallels found in the Egyptian hymns of victory. The victory hymn of Thutmosis III offers a particularly full parallel to 2 Samuel 7. It is introduced as the words of Amon-Re and recounts how he promoted the king's career (cf. 2 Sam. 7:8ff.), giving him victory over all Egypt's inveterate enemies on every side (cf. 2 Sam. 7:1, 11, 23). It then states that the king has erected the god's dwelling place (cf. 2 Sam. 7:2, 13) and affirms that the god has established the king on his throne forever (cf. 2 Sam. 7:11-16).

It is particularly noteworthy that the idea that a temple should be built for Yahweh, if not by the victorious David at least by his son (2 Sam. 7:13), would fit as an authentic element in the ancient literary pattern. To that extent the extensive parallel outlined above supports the integrity of verse 13 against the common rejection of it as a harmonizing addition by a later editor. Also supportive of the originality of verse 13 is the lyric reflection of the 2 Samuel 7 episode in Psalm 132. For in this psalm the king's building of a habitation for Yahweh is a central feature in Yahweh's establishment of David's dynasty by oath.[7]

In an adaptation of the victory hymn of Thutmosis III found in the building inscription of Amenophis III, the words of Amon-Re to the king follow the king's description of the temple monuments which he has made for the god. Here, then, the close interrelationship of the themes of victory and temple-building is made particularly apparent.

The composition of 2 Samuel 7 as an oracle of Yahweh joined with the prayer response of David should be compared with the blend of words of god and king addressed to one another in the stele of Amenophis III.[8] The oracle also has its parallels in the suzerainty treaties which

[7] Cf. R. de Vaux, "Jerusalem and the Prophets," in *Interpreting the Prophetic Tradition* (ed. H. Orlinsky; New York, 1969), p. 278. On the integrity of verse 13, cf. A. Caquot, "La prophétie de Nathan et ses échos lyriques," in *International Organization for the Study of the Old Testament, Congress Volume, Bonn, 1962: Supplements to Vetus Testamentum*, IX (Leiden, 1963), 213ff.

[8] Kitchen (*New Perspectives on the Old Testament* [ed. J. B. Payne; Waco, 1970], p. 8) observes that the most characteristic elements of this triumphal speech pattern continued from the fifteenth to the tenth centuries B.C. in Egyptian literary tradition, which is roughly equivalent to the period in which we have traced it in the Old Testament above.

promise prolongation of dynasty to the vassal king. [9] These parallels consist in formal similarities in ideology and concept. But as an oracle of God in the context of David's military triumphs, the structural form of Nathan's words is to be compared with the Egyptian victory hymns. When we consider that this covenant with David was to be consummated in the divine scion, Christ the Lord, we can appreciate the appropriateness of this fusion of treaty tradition with a literary form which gave expression to an ideology of divine kingship.

Channeled through the Davidic covenant, the history of Yahweh's triumphantly royal house-building reached forward to the age of the new covenant. At that time the temple of God in its antitypical form would be raised up and Scripture would again play the same architectural role as of old.

We are following representations in the New Testament itself when we identify the Scripture of the new covenant as the triumphant architectural word of the risen and exalted Saviour. Having vanquished the Satanic dragon (cf. Rev. 12:1ff.), Christ was invested with cosmic authority and proceeded according to the Old Testament paradigm to build his royal residence. In this Messianic son of David the dynastic house firmly established by God's covenant with David culminated; he is the son of David who builds the true and eternal house of God. Surpassing the intimations of the ancient oracle, he not only builds but himself is the true temple of God. In the "body" of Christ, according to the New Testament revelation concerning the incarnation of the Son and the mystery-union of his people with him in the Spirit as God's holy dwelling (cf. 1 Pet. 2:5), there occurs the ultimate transmutation of the temple of God.

Now redemptive eschatology is a complex development, and prior to the consummation the Messianic

[9] Cf. P. J. Calderone, *Dynastic Oracle and Suzerainty Treaty* (Manila, 1966). Cf., too, *TGK*, pp. 36ff.

temple exists as an organization with principles of incorporation and with an authority structure and program appropriate to its existence in this world as one historical institution among others. In this respect, there is, in spite of great differences, a similarity between the house of the new covenant community over which Christ is set as Son and the old covenant house over which Moses was set as servant (Heb. 3:2-6). And the words of the New Testament which the enthroned Christ has spoken through his inspired ministers of the new covenant are his architectural directives for the holy task of constructing this new covenant house. The New Testament is the triumphant Lord's house-building word, his architectonic covenant for the new Israel.

In terms of its edificatory purpose, covenantal canon may be thought of as the architectural model for God's sanctuary-residence. The functional essence of biblical canon is thus imaged in that series of divinely revealed sanctuary plans which began with the tabernacle plan delineated by God for Moses in the mount (Exod. 25ff.; cf. Heb. 8:5).[10] This was followed by the temple design given to David and by him transmitted to Solomon (1 Chron. 28, esp. v. 19). A visionary model of the eschatological temple was revealed to Ezekiel on the high mountain (Ezek. 40ff.), the ordinances pertaining to it being called "the law of the house" (Ezek. 43:12). And finally there was the revelation of the eternal temple-city given to the apostle John, again in a vision beheld from a great, high mountain (Rev. 21:10ff.).[11]

[10] The most familiar example of this sort of thing from extra-biblical sources is found on the Gudea cylinders. It is there narrated that Gudea in a dream beheld Nindub, the architect god, draw a plan on a lapis lazuli tablet for the temple-house Eninnu, which this Sumerian ruler was to build for Ningirsu, tutelary deity of Lagash.

[11] This temple model stands in close conjunction with John's striking use of the canonical sanction derived from the treaty tradition (Rev. 22:18ff.).

The apocalyptic temple-city seen by John imparts a distinctly architectural cast to the new heaven and new earth of which it is the glory (Rev. 21:1ff.). The eschatological re-creation event is thus a divine house-building, and the account of it appropriately follows immediately after that of the final judgment-conquest of the dragon and his hosts (Rev. 20:10; cf. v. 2), by which the son of David secured rest forever from all the enemies round about.[12]

Now since the manifest intent in the depiction of the eternal house of God in Revelation 21 and 22 is to present it as the restored and consummated paradise of God, we are led to recognize that the first creating of heaven and earth was also a process of divine house-building—the original construction of a dwelling place for God. The creation process is thus viewed from a house-building perspective in Proverbs 8:22ff. also. There wisdom is the architect (so, according to one reasonable interpretation of the 'āmôn of v. 30) in the day by day triumphs of creation. As this passage continues there is an explicit reference to the house wisdom builds, with possibly an allusion to the seven-day structure of the creation history (cf. also Ps. 93, esp. vv. 2 and 5).[13] Other instances of the association of wisdom with the building of God's house may be noted in passing. Wisdom as vocational gift plays a prominent role in the histories of both the Mosaic tabernacle and the Solomonic temple in the figures of the wise craftsmen Bezalel (Exod. 31:2ff.;

[12] The same sequence is found in the Ezekiel background of Revelation 20. Immediately before the prophecy of the new temple in the new paradise land (Ezek. 40-48) is that of the judgment of the great enemy, described in terms of God's conquest of the dragon (Ezek. 38, 39). Cf. H. G. May, "Cosmological Reference in the Qumran Doctrine of the Two Spirits and in Old Testament Imagery," *Journal of Biblical Literature*, LXXXII, 1 (1963), 8f.

[13] Similar creation perspectives can be detected in the prologue of John.

35:30ff.) and the Tyrian Huram-abi (2 Chron. 2:13).[14]
The themes of Solomon's own reception of wisdom and
his temple-planning are closely related in 1 Kings 3-5.[15]

In the original creation record of Genesis 1:1-2:3, the
triumph (or at least the display of God's absolute sovereignty) and the house-building are concurrent aspects of
the one creation process. The vast deep-and-darkness
which God first created he then bounded and structured
until the divine design for creation was realized that it
should not be a chaos but a habitation (Isa. 45:18). In
the midst of the earth stood the holy garden of God, his
microcosmic royal sanctuary, the dwelling place into
which he received the God-like earthling to serve as
princely gardener and priestly guardian. Then the Creator
enthroned himself in his cosmic house, the heaven his
throne, the earth his footstool; on the seventh day he sat
as king in the archetypal place of his rest (Isa. 66:1).

Such was the long-historied ideological pattern to
which Scripture from its first appearance belonged as an
integrally functioning part.[16] This portrayal of Scripture
according to the architectural image which it suggests for
itself highlights that constitutional function of the Bible
which comes to the front and center as soon as Scripture
is recognized as covenant document. Thus viewed as

[14] For comparison of Solomon's recourse to the Tyrian artisan
with Baal's employing of Kothar-and-Hasis of Crete to build his
royal house, see C. H. Gordon, *Ugarit and Minoan Crete* (New
York, 1966), pp. 22f.

[15] We may also note the thesis that the wisdom book of
Proverbs was so designed that its layout in the columns of the
scroll represented "wisdom's house" (Prov. 9:1), this house being
in certain respects like Solomon's temple, whose vertical dimensions it followed. So P. W. Skehan, "Wisdom's House," *Catholic
Biblical Quarterly*, XXIX (1967), 468-486.

[16] In connection with the essential role of treaty canon as
instrument for building God's house, we may recall again the
ark-enshrinement of the Lord's treaty within his sanctuary-house,
and the designation of the Sefireh treaty texts as "bethels" (cf.
TGK, p. 44).

treaty documents, the Old and New Testaments have the specific purpose of serving as a building plan for the community structure of God's covenant people. The function of each Testament as a legal, administrative document is primarily to define the covenant community as an authority structure or system of government by which the lordship of Yahweh-Christ is actualized among his servant people.

Community Correlative to Biblical Canon

When it comes to the church's proclamation of the biblical message and to the systematic reformulation of the data of the Scriptures for dogmatic theology, what the Bible reveals about God himself and the salvation he has wrought and now offers to men will, of course, be the central and paramount themes. But, however far-ranging and sublime the contents of the Old and New Testaments, in the formal atomic unity of each Testament as a covenant document everything orbits about its nuclear architectural-governmental function.

The community-structuring identification of canonical Scripture calls for a reassessment of the relationship of community and canon. In this connection it is first necessary to notice that there are two different ways in which Scripture functions as God's house-building instrument. These two ways correspond to the distinction between the Scriptures as authoritative word and as powerful word. As word of power, Scripture finds a prototype in the original, creation house-building of God. The divine creative fiats were God's effectual architectural utterances by which he actually produced and actively manipulated ultimate materials—light, life, and spirit—so fashioning his creation house. Similarly, the Scriptural word of God effectually wielded by the Spirit is the fiat of God's new creation.[17] It is through the instrumentali-

---

[17] The biblical interpretation of God's covenantal dealings with

ty of Scripture as powerful word that God constructs his new redemptive temple-house, dynamically molding and incorporating his people as living stones into this holy structure. So employed by the Spirit, Scripture is architectural fiat.

In our study of canon, our concern is with Scripture not as powerful word but as authoritative word, not as architectural fiat but as architectonic model. For canonicity is a matter of authoritative norms. Thus, when we affirm that the Old Testament is the canonical covenant by which the Lord built the kingdom-house of Israel, we refer to the fact that God structured the covenant community preceptively by the covenant stipulations[18] and definitively delineated the constituent elements of his holy house in its historical and theological, human and divine dimensions. As to its nuclear formal function, canonical covenant is a community rule.

Inasmuch, then, as canonical Scripture is God's house-building word, the community rule for his covenant people, the Reformation insistence is confirmed that the Scriptures form the church, and not vice versa. Indeed, in respect to the formal identity of Scripture, that position turns out to be true in an even more precise way than Reformed orthodoxy has had in mind. Yet, curiously, we are at the same time compelled by this apprehension of the nature of biblical canon as constitution for the com-

Israel as a new work of creation is evident in the terminology and the choice of literary motifs in the historical narratives describing that relationship and in the hymnic and prophetic treatments of it (as, e.g., in Ps. 74 and Isa. 43).

[18] The precepts may be prophetic (e.g., the Deuteronomic stipulations concerning the future king or the central altar at its permanent site) and, since Scripture cannot be broken, such prophetic laws inevitably prove to be fiat as well as norm. Indeed, since the law of God's house in general is the word of triumphant Yahweh and is accompanied by the sure prophecy that God's house will be built, the authoritative word must ever prove to be the powerful word too. Scripture must become architectural fiat; but it is antecedently architectural model.

munity to acknowledge that our traditional formulations of the canon doctrine have not done full justice to the role of the community.

The community is inextricably bound up in the reality of canonical Scripture. The concept of covenant-canon requires a covenant community. Though the community does not confer canonical authority on the Scriptures, Scripture in the form of constitutional treaty implies the community constituted by it and existing under its authority. Canonical authority is not derived from community, but covenantal canon connotes covenantal community.[19]

This correlative status of the community confronts us again as we analyze further the nature of the covenant documents of which the canonical Scriptures are an adaptation. Such a document was in effect the vassal's oath of allegiance recorded. The treaty text was a documentary witness to his covenant oath. The actual oath-malediction sworn by the vassal in the ratification ceremony might be contained in the treaty document,[20] but whether or not this ritual response was cited in the text, the legal character of the document was that of sacred witness to the vassal's commitment. Accordingly, a treaty was at one and the same time a declaration of the

[19] Wright (*op. cit.*, pp. 179f.) regards it as probable that the idea of canon had its roots in ceremonial renewals of the Mosaic covenant by the Israelite community. To that extent there is a certain formal correspondence between his view of the history of the canon and that of the present study. However, in his reconstruction the force of the new insights is resisted. The traditional critical outlook is still clearly dominant in his judgment that the canon concept did not come to full development until the post-exilic community accepted the law from Ezra as their constitution. Moreover, Wright's view of the role of the community in relation to the canon is radically different from the one adopted above (see further below, Part I, Ch. 4).

[20] See *TGK*, p. 29, and my "Abram's Amen," *Westminster Theological Journal*, XXXI, 1 (1968), 3.

suzerain's authority and an attestation to the authority of his treaty words by the vassal.

Inherent, therefore, in the covenantal nature of the foundational Old Testament documents was Israel's acknowledgment of their canonical authority. In the extension of the covenantal canon beyond the Mosaic treaties this aspect of community attestation surfaces here and there, especially, as we have noticed, in the Psalter with its confessional responses to God's covenantal law and gospel. Hence, the modern approach that would define canon in terms of the community's acceptance of certain books is seen to be divorced from historical-literary reality when it posits a late "canonization" of the Old Testament, even judging this viewpoint on the basis of its own definition of canon. For the Old Testament as covenantal canon was by nature community-attested canon from the time of its Mosaic beginnings.

A parallel between certain biblical and extrabiblical treaties may be cited in illustration of this community-attested character of covenant documents. The Aramaic treaty text, Sefireh I, was prepared by the vassal, Mati'el.[21] Commenting on the purpose of this stele with its treaty inscription, the vassal observes[22] that it was designed as a memorial for his successors, so that adhering to its demands the dynasty might endure, not suffering the treaty curses. Comparable is the second set of Decalogue treaty tablets, which, in distinction from the divinely originated first copies, was prepared by Moses (Exod. 34:1a).[23] Insofar as Moses was acting as representative of the vassal people Israel in this cove-

[21] The meaning of the text (line 2) is probably that Mati'el had a scribe engrave the inscription on the stele. Cf. J. A. Fitzmyer, *The Aramaic Inscriptions of Sefîre* (Rome, 1967), p. 73.

[22] The observation is found in conjunction with an inscriptional clause on face C.

[23] Apparently God himself inscribed these as he had the originals (cf. Exod. 34:1b, 28b and, with respect to the originals, Exod. 24:12; 31:18; 32:16).

nantal engagement, the tablets thus produced to be inscribed with the treaty might be construed, like the treaty prepared by the vassal Mati'el, as Israel's own memorial witness against itself. This was explicitly so in the case of the Deuteronomic treaty, which was also vassal-produced.[24] For according to Moses' charge to the Levitical guardians of the covenantal "book of the law," it was to be placed by the ark of the covenant that it might "be there for a witness against you" (Deut. 31:26).[25]

Within the Deuteronomic treaty the vassal-witness aspect of the treaty is given fullest and clearest expression in the Mosaic Song of Witness (Deut. 32). The Lord instructed Moses to teach the people this Song that it might be in their mouths and in the mouths of their descendants as their own witness for Yahweh and against themselves (Deut. 31:19ff.). Like Mati'el's statement concerning the memorial purpose of the copy of the treaty he prepared, the Mosaic Song of Witness appears in context with the Deuteronomic treaty's inscriptional clause (cf. Deut. 31:9ff. and 24ff.) and is expressly concerned with the ongoing vassal generations (cf. Deut. 31:21; 32:46) and their avoidance of the threatened evils.

The oral transmission history of the Song of Witness was thus a process of confession by Israel that the treaty Scripture to which the Song belonged and whose sanctions it amplified was canonically determinative of their destiny. With this Song in their mouths, the continuing servant people Israel constituted generation after generation a living sign of attestation to the divine origin and authority of the covenantal Scriptures. The authenticating force of the wonder-signs wrought by Moses before

[24] See Deuteronomy 31:9, 24 for the preparation of the Deuteronomic treaty text by Moses.

[25] Cf. the Joshua 24:26 record of Joshua's writing of the words of Israel's renewed covenantal witness against themselves (v. 22) in "the book of the law of God."

the eyes of this covenant community at its founding was
caught up and perpetuated in that living witness to Yahweh's canonical words, reproduced and echoed on the
lips of children's children.

Chapter Four

CANONICAL POLITIES, OLD AND NEW

The identification of the Old-New Testament schema with the pattern of treaty-documented covenant renewal attested in ancient international diplomacy[1] establishes the formal perspective for an approach to the question of the discontinuity between the Old and New Testaments and, more specifically, to the question of the relation of the Old Testament to the canon of the Christian church.

Old Canon in the New Covenant

In respect to the permanence of canonicity, an analogue to the biblical situation is found in the administration of the ancient political treaties. These treaties spoke of the alliances they founded and the terms they stipulated as valid down through following generations indefinitely. So, for example, the copies of the Bir-Ga'yah treaty with Mati'el speak in various connections of its arrangements, sanctions, and the suzerain's authority as being "forever."[2] Nevertheless, these treaties were under

[1] See above, pp. 68ff.

[2] So also both Egyptian and Hittite versions of the parity treaty between Ramses II and Hattusilis declare repeatedly that that treaty of peace and brotherhood was valid "forever."

the sovereign disposition of the great king and subject to his revision. As has been previously noted, the treaty provisions might be altered because of changing circumstances in the development of the covenant relationship.[3] Treaty alterations of a more general type would attend the preparation of the new documents in the process of covenant renewal.[4] Such renewals gave expression at once to the (at least theoretically) eternal character of these treaties and to the fact that the covenant order was not static but correlated to historical movement and change. The legal compatibility of these two aspects, the eternal and the changing, must have resided in a recognition of a distinction between the fundamental tributary allegiance of the vassal to the great king (or the mutual peaceful stance of the partners to a parity treaty), which was theoretically and ideally permanent, and the precise details, such as boundary definitions and tribute specifications, etc., which were subject to alteration.[5]

The canonical covenants in the Bible are similarly "forever" yet subject to change. The relationship established by God with his people and progressively unfolded toward a predestined consummation as portrayed in Scripture is an eternal covenant relationship. This covenant order, however, is subject to the Lord Yahweh, who according to his sovereign purposes directs and forwards

[3] See above, p. 54.

[4] See above, p. 69, n. 54.

[5] Baltzer (*op. cit.*) distinguishes in the treaty structure between a declaration of basic principle and the specific stipulations that follow it. The variations among the three Sefireh steles, which describe the treaty relationship they record as "forever" valid, show how the concept of covenant permanence was compatible with a degree of difference in detail even in contemporary versions of the same treaty. (For discussion, see McCarthy, *op. cit.*, pp. 62f., and Fitzmyer, *op. cit.*, pp. 2f., 79, and 94.) Such variations are of importance, too, for a study of scribal freedom, of interest to the biblical scholar as a possible explanation of textual variations in parallel passages without recourse to easy assumptions of transmissional mutation.

redemption's eschatological development by decisive interventions, initiating distinctive new eras and authoritatively redefining the mode of his kingdom. These advances and renewals with their alterations of previous arrangements are certified in the continuing Scriptural documentation of the covenant.

Reluctance to accept the reality of God's sovereignty in history as expressed in this divine structuring of the redemptive process into eschatological epochs underlies the misguided modern analyses that view the discontinuity between Old and New Testaments in simplistically evolutional fashion and judge not a little in the Old Testament to be sub-Christian.[6] On the other extreme, interpretations of a dispensational brand, while quite insistent on the fact of divinely differentiated eras, misconstrue the discontinuity aspect of the redemptive process, positing such radical disjunctions between the successive eras that a genuine continuity between the Old and New Testaments becomes insolubly problematic. The actual covenantal continuity-discontinuity pattern of the Old and New Testaments does not come into its own in either evolutional or dispensational historiography, and in the measure that that is so the question of the authority of the Old Testament in the Christian church cannot be properly assessed. The danger of having our position misunderstood as fostering the errors of one or both of these viewpoints ought not deter us from drawing out its implications.

What, then, does follow from the identification of the canonicity of the Old and New Testaments as covenantal canonicity, and the recognition that these covenants are at once "forever" and yet subject to revision? For one thing, Scripture should not be thought of as a closed

6 For a fairly recent popular restatement of this viewpoint in connection with a discussion of the canon question and from an ecclesiastically significant source, see F. V. Filson, *Which Books Belong in the Bible?* (Philadelphia, 1957), pp. 52ff.

canon in some vaguely absolute sense, as though biblical canonicity were something unqualifiedly permanent. In fact, if biblical canon is covenantal canon and there are in the composition of the Bible two covenants, one old and one new, there are also two canons, one old and one new. Instead of speaking of the canon of Scripture, we should then speak of the Old and New Testament canons, or of the canonical covenants which constitute the Scripture.

Each inscripturated covenant is closed to alteration, subtraction, or addition by the vassals (as the proscriptions of the treaty document clauses insist); yet each is open to revision by the Suzerain, revision that does not destroy but fulfills, as the history of God's kingdom proceeds from one epochal stage to the next, particularly in the passage from the old covenant to the new. Each authoritative covenantal corpus is of fixed extent, but the historical order for which it is the constitution is not a perpetually closed system. Each canon is of divine authority in all its parts, but its norms may not be automatically absolutized in abstraction from the covenantally structured historical process. Together the old and new covenant canons share in redemption's eschatological movement with its pattern of renewal, of promise and Messianic fulfillment, the latter in semi-eschatological and consummate stages. "Closed" as a general description of a canon would be suitable only in the eternal state of the consummation.

The identity of the Old and New Testaments as two distinct canons and the integrity of each Testament in itself as a separate canonical whole are underscored by the conclusion we have previously reached that the function each Testament performs as an architectural model for a particular community structure is its nuclear, identifying function. As polities for two different covenant orders, the Mosaic and the Messianic, the two covenantal canons stand over against one another, each in its own individual literary-legal unity and completeness.

They are, of course, indissolubly bound to one another in organic spiritual-historical relationship. They both unfold the same principle of redemptive grace, moving forward to a common eternal goal in the city of God. The blessings of old and new orders derive from the very same works of satisfaction accomplished by the Christ of God, and where spiritual life is found in either order it is attributable to the creative action of the one and selfsame Spirit of Christ. According to the divine design the old is provisional and preparatory for the new, and by divine predisclosure the new is prophetically anticipated in the old. External event and institution in the old order were divinely fashioned to afford a systematic representation of the realities of the coming new order, so producing a type-antitype correlativity between the two covenants in which their unity is instructively articulated.

The continuity between them is evident even in the area of their distinctive formal polities. For when we reckon with the invisible dimension of the New Testament order, specifically with the heavenly kingship of the glorified Christ over his church, we perceive that the governmental structure of the New Testament order like that of the old Israel is a theocratic monarchy. A dynastic linkage gives further expression to this continuity, for the heavenly throne which Christ occupies is the throne of David in its archetypal pattern and its antitypical perfection.[7]

Nevertheless, at the level of its visible structure there are obvious and important differences between the new covenant community and the old organization of God's people. The full significance of these differences between the cultural-cultic kingdom of Israel and the church of

[7] The continuity between the old and new orders in the area of polity extends to various other aspects of their organization as well, such as the policy of incorporation into the membership of the covenant community on the basis of the authority principle (cf. *BOC*, pp. 84ff.).

Christ, which is strictly cultic in the present phase of its visible functioning,[8] must be duly appreciated. When full weight is given to these differences, the Old and New Testaments, which respectively define and establish these two structures, will be clearly seen as two separate and distinct architectural models for the house of God in two quite separate and distinct stages of its history. The distinctiveness of the two community organizations brings out the individual integrity of the two Testaments which serve as community rules for the two orders. The Old and New Testaments are two discrete covenant polities, and since biblical canon is covenantal polity-canon, they are two discrete canons in series.

This is to say that the Old Testament is not the canon of the Christian church. Covenant Theology is completely biblical in its insistence on the Christological unity of the Covenant of Redemption as both law and gospel in its old and new administrations.[9] But the old covenant is not the new covenant. The form of government appointed in the old covenant is not the community polity for the church of the new covenant, its ritual legislation is not a directory for the church's cultic practice, nor can the program of conquest it prescribes be equated with the evangelistic mission of the church in this world.[10]

A distinction thus arises for the Christian church between canon and Scripture. In drawing such a distinction we should at once set off our position from the modern one with a similar sound. A recent statement of this

[8] Cf. *BOC*, pp. 99ff.

[9] Cf. *ibid.*, Chapter 2.

[10] The broader programmatic and ethical compatibility of the old and new orders will not be discerned apart from an uncritically objective reading of the biblical revelation concerning the eschatological structuring of the history of God's kingdom with its complex of divinely defined, interrelated epochs. I would still subscribe to the basic thesis of my early effort to analyze this matter in "The Intrusion and the Decalogue," *Westminster Theological Journal,* XVI, 1 (1953), 1-22 (see below, Part II, Ch. 3).

current approach is provided by Wright.[11] He speaks of a
canon within the canon, or within Scripture. So far is his
distinction from the one being made here, however, that
he repeats the wearisome charge of bibliolatry against the
kind of reverence for Scripture that informs the latter.
Wright identifies the canon within the canon with those
parts of the Bible regarded as most important and relevant by the theology of a particular historical moment.
He recognizes the relativism of his position but somehow
fails to perceive that his characteristically critical interpretation of the relation of community tradition to
canonical Scripture precludes a genuine canonicity of the
Bible by effectively muffling the divine voice of authority
speaking therein, and thus is itself the real idolatry.

An attempt is made by Childs[12] to get beyond canon-
within-the-canon approaches. He is critical of identifying
the unity of the Bible in terms of centripetal forces
abstracted from the Bible's total diversity. His thesis is
that the context for doing biblical theology is the Christian church's canon as such. Nevertheless, Childs fails to
show how he could avoid being forced to acknowledge a
canon within the canon, or a limited unity of the Bible.
For no more than those he criticizes does he want to
return to an orthodox confession of the infallibility of
Scripture. Indeed, his approach cannot in the last analysis
provide for objective Scriptural authority at all, since, in
his adoption of a Barthian view of the role of the respon-
sive community in the inspiration process, he has made
human subjectivity constitutive in canonical authority.

Our thesis that there is a distinction between the
Scriptures and the canon of the Christian church involves
no such denial of biblical infallibility. It simply asserts
that the treaty canon that governs the church of the new
covenant as a formal community is the New Testament
alone, while Scripture is the broader entity consisting of

11 *Op. cit.*, pp. 180ff.
12 B. S. Childs, *Biblical Theology in Crisis* (Philadelphia, 1970).

the canonical oracles of God communicated to his people in both Mosaic and Messianic eras, the Old and New Testaments together.

In the framework of the thoroughgoing spiritual-eschatological unity of all the redemptive administrations of God's kingdom, the character of all Scripture as equally the word of God commands for the Old Testament Scripture the place it has actually held in the faithful church from the beginning. It is able to make wise unto salvation through faith in Jesus Christ. It is profitable for doctrine, reproof, correction, and instruction in righteousness. As Scriptural revelation the Old Testament provides norms for faith. Indeed, all that the Old Testament teaches concerning God and the history of his relationship to his creation is normative for Christian faith. Its historical record, preredemptive and redemptive, is altogether truthful. The New Testament revelation of God's saving acts through Christ presupposes and cannot be adequately comprehended apart from the world-view presented in the Old Testament and the disclosures found there concerning man as a creature living before the face of his Creator, first in the normalcy of the covenant in Eden and since the Fall in the abnormality of a state of exile in the earth, yet with a call to restoration within the fellowship of an elect and redeemed remnant community. Likewise the faith-norms of the Old Testament pertaining to the operation of the principles of law and grace in man's salvation continue to be normative for faith in the New Testament revelation. In the nature of the case, all the faith-norm content of the Old Testament remains authoritative for faith in all ages.

If to be normative for faith were what qualified for canonical status, the Old Testament would belong to the canon of the Christian church. However, the *sine qua non* of biblical canonicity, canonicity of the covenantal type, is not a matter of faith-norms but of life-norms. More specifically, inasmuch as the nuclear function of each canonical Testament is to structure the polity of the

covenant people, canonicity precisely and properly defined is a matter of *community* life-norms.

There are, of course, life-norms found in the Old
Testament which continue to be authoritative standards
of human conduct in New Testament times. Such, for
example, are the creation ordinances of marriage and
labor, instituted in Eden, reinstituted after the Fall, and
covenantally formalized in the postdiluvian covenant
which God made with all the earth, explicitly for as long
as the earth should endure. Such, too, are the universally
applicable individual life-norms included in the stipulations of the Mosaic covenants, regulative of a man's life in
relation to his neighbor. The New Testament, though not
legislatively codifying these life-norms, does presuppose
them and didactically confirm them.

But the Old Testament's community life-norms for
Israel are replaced in the New Testament by a new polity
for the church. The Old Testament laws dealing with the
institutional mode of the kingdom of God in relation to
the cultural mandate and with the community cultus of
Israel, those norms which are the peculiarly canonical
norms, were binding only on the community of the old
covenant. In these terms, the Old Testament, though
possessing the general authority of all the Scriptures, does
not possess for the church the more specific authority of
canonicity. Under the new covenant the Old Testament is
not the current canon.

Intracanonical Polity Phases

When we have thus observed that the Old Testament
does not provide the organizational constitution for the
church of the new covenant and is not, therefore, canonical for the church, we have made the major distinction
that must be made within Scripture in this regard. But
the determination of what biblical content is currently
normative, even in the canonically significant area of
polity, is more involved than that. For within the Old

Testament canon itself distinct stages are legislatively delineated for the developing form of community government—and a similar situation obtains in the New Testament. Hence not all that is contained in Old Testament laws concerning Israelite institutions was intended to be normative in all periods of Israel's history.

In prescribing the structure of God's kingdom-house and of his cultic-house, Pentateuchal law had to address itself to three clearly demarcated stages in Israel's development. The first was the foundational but preliminary wilderness phase extending from the covenant-making at Sinai to the Transjordanian conquests under Moses. The second was the transitional stage from the Joshuan penetration of Canaan through the unsettled centuries of settlement under the judges. The third era arrived with the monarchy and particularly with the rise of David when Israel secured rest from the enemies of the kingdom round about. With this last development the Old Testament theocratic form attained maturity or permanence, of an Old Testament sort. Of course, when account is taken of the nature of the whole Old Testament age as preparatory for the coming of the Messianic days, it appears that the permanence of even Israel's monarchical stage was only relative.

The laws of the Mosaic covenants were programmed from the outset for this succession of modifications in Israel's polity. So, for example, Moses not only prescribed arrangements for the administration of justice during his own leadership of Israel, but appointed a modified judicial system to meet the new conditions that would presently obtain upon the entry into Canaan (Deut. 16:18ff.); and for the more distant future, he incorporated into the Deuteronomic treaty the law of the king (Deut. 17:14ff.).[13] Precepts dealing with the future, near or remote, were potentially effective, becoming normative when Yahweh had brought to pass the situa-

[13] Cf. *TGK*, pp. 94ff.

tion which those precepts legislatively anticipated. When a later phase with its modified norms arrived, the prescriptions peculiarly designed for an earlier phase naturally ceased to be normative. The secret of the ability of biblical canon to preordain institutional changes through the coming centuries of the covenant community's development was the Spirit of prophecy.[14] Modern higher criticism's repudiation of such prophetic precept has certainly been the compelling reason for its later dating of Mosaic legislation, even if other arguments have often been more conspicuously adduced.

In addition to legislating for the three distinct eras that followed the organization of the kingdom of Israel at Sinai (the particular kingdom order for which the Old Testament Scriptures served as covenant canon), the Old Testament narrates the pre-Sinaitic relationships of God and his people. Although part of Israel's canon, this narrative material tracing the prehistory of the covenant community back to the earliest covenantal arrangements between the Creator and man functions within the Old Testament canon not as legislation but as historical prologue.[15] Not that this prologue does not contain preceptive material; it prescribes the governmental structure of covenant communities (Adamic, Noahic, Abrahamic) in various degrees of continuity with post-Sinaitic Israel. Nevertheless, these pre-Sinaitic (including even preredemptive) covenantal polities found within the prologue's historical survey were in major respects unlike the kingdom form of Israel and there is no question of thinking

[14] Besides prescribing prophetically for its own several polity phases, the Old Testament foretells significant New Testament polity developments, such as the universalism of the Messianic community. Such prophecies, however, do not function legislatively in the Old Testament canon but judicially, expounding and enforcing the eschatological sanctions of the old covenant rather than elaborating its stipulations.

[15] See above, p. 53.

of them as currently normative for the community which at Sinai began to receive the Old Testament canon.[16]

In brief, the Old Testament canon was given as the covenant constitution for the Israelite community formally established as a kingdom under Moses, the servant of Yahweh. The ground layer of this canon bears witness to the covenant-making events by which that kingdom was established, and it includes besides, as an historical prelude, a record of prior relationships of the parties to the treaty, or their predecessors, back to the very beginnings. Then in its legislation for the Mosaic kingdom the Old Testament canon spans a series of preappointed stages in community structure down to the final, Davidic phase of Old Testament polity. Consequently, among the regulations relating to the institutional structure of this kingdom there are some which were of temporally limited authority.

However, though not all the polity prescriptions for Israel were currently normative at all times even within the Old Testament era, they do all possess an inner coherence as belonging to a single general type, a peculiar institutional integration of culture and cult. The successive Old Testament stages of the kingdom were designed to arrive at a fully matured form of this general type, all the institutional modifications remaining within the limits of this type. Hence, even though canonicity is a matter of community life-norms, or polities, the contents of the Old Testament are not to be subdivided into several canons according to their relation to the several stages in

[16] Or stating a corollary, the Old Testament covenantal canon was not the treaty document for these earlier covenant administrations. That would apply all the more to the postdiluvian covenant of God with the earth (Gen. 9), even though that covenant, intact, continued to be in force into post-Sinaitic times and even into the New Testament age. Hence, also, the mere presence of an account of such a continuing covenant in Old Testament historical narrative has no relevance for the question of the Old Testament's canonicity in New Testament times.

Israel's polity. As over against the New Testament structure of the church, the Old Testament kingdom throughout the course of Israel's changing polity exhibits its own
peculiar stamp. Correspondingly, the Old Testament
canon possesses an integral unity over against the New
Testament canon, each of these covenantal literary com-
plexes being a discrete canonical whole.

The same kind of complexity that was found in the
Old Testament characterizes the New Testament data on
community polity. In the gospels the New Testament
canon testifies to the covenant-making events which were
foundational to the building of the house of God over
which Jesus was set as a Son. Then beyond the gospels
the New Testament reflects a history of church polity
involving distinct stages.

As in the Old Testament, following the founding ministry of the covenant mediator there was a transitional era
of community extension for the church. In the Old
Testament, this period witnessed a movement of the
covenant people from outside of Canaan into the land
and eventually to a central cultic focus at Jerusalem,
Yahweh's selection of which for his permanent residence
fully introduced the final Old Testament stage of polity.
In the New Testament this era was marked by a reverse
movement, from the disengagement of the sanctuary of
God from Jerusalem to the expansion of God's people
among the nations. A special polity marked this transitional phase, one in which the church was directed by the
apostles of the Lord.

With the passing of the apostolic generation came the
stable, permanent stage of church order—"permanent"
once again in a relative sense since this stage also is to be
terminated in the consummation of the present course of
history at the coming of the covenant Lord.[17] The intro-

[17] The consummation order to be established by Christ at his
coming is actually the final and truly permanent stage of the new
covenant. However, since Scriptural canon is surely a mode of

duction of the final New Testament polity did not require the emergence of some new governmental agency (like the monarchy in the final Old Testament stage), for the ultimate structure already existed within the special apostolic order and after the latter's gradual disappearance simply continued on (from a normative point of view, at least) as the permanent polity of the church.

In the prelude to the gospels' record of the Messiah's covenant-ratifying sacrifice, the New Testament deals with a prechurch order too. The mission of John the Baptist and, as to its immediate design, the ministry of Jesus narrated there fell within the climactic, closing days of that old covenant order from within which the new covenant community was emerging. Moreover, this old covenant order was actually to be perpetuated for a generation after the inauguration of the new age with its new community—the generation during which the New Testament canon was produced.

Consequently, determining what is currently normative within the New Testament canon for community structure and function involves a process of discrimination analogous to that which faced those living under the Old Testament canon.[18] Although the New Testament canon is the currently normative canon for the church, it contains in the gospels certain directives for the company of Jesus' disciples which were applicable only within the old covenant order, and elsewhere in the New Testament

revelation belonging to this world and not to the next, the present era of the new covenant is the last one for which the New Testament canon serves as polity norm, or, for that matter, the last one for which the subject of Scriptural canon has current relevance.

[18] An important difference between the two situations is that Israel's interpreting of canonical norms was facilitated through most of her history by the provision of continuing special revelation, the growth of the old canon itself covering about a millennium. In contrast, the creation of the canon of the New Testament church was confined to one generation, with a concomitant temporal limitation of other forms of special revelation.

directives are found which were made temporarily expedient by that overlapping of the old and new orders which was not terminated until the judgment of the former in A.D. 70.

So, for example, certain procedural details of the mission of the twelve (see Matt. 10:1ff.; Mark 6:7ff.; Luke 9:1ff.)[19] or the mission of the seventy (Luke 10:1ff.) were conditioned by their old order context and hence are not normative for the present mission of the church. Examples of transitional features explicable in terms of the temporary overlapping of the covenants but no longer normative are the Jerusalem council's ruling concerning certain Old Testament cultic proscriptions (Acts 15:20, 29) and the more positive endorsement of the continuing legitimacy of the Jerusalem temple cultus by the practice of the apostles (cf., e.g., Acts 21:24).

There is the further necessity to distinguish current from noncurrent norms which arises from the fact that the New Testament prescribes for more than one phase of church polity as it renders canonical service for apostolic and postapostolic eras. For example, it is within the framework of the church's distinctive phases, and particularly with due regard for the special historical purposes of the apostolic phase of the new order, that the interpretation of the church's early charismatic functions must be sought.

Before the summarizing conclusion, one brief observation may be allowed, noting a specific consequence of our thesis for the doctrine of the church. Our investigation speaks decisively against every tendency to regard the church as amorphous fellowship and mission. Such is not the way of God's administration of his covenant through history. The proper nature of the covenant community as a visible authority structure, under the new covenant as under the old, is proclaimed by the very

---

[19] Cf. the limitation of Jesus' activity to the Israelite tribes (Matt. 15:24).

identity of the canonical Word of God addressed to that community: an architectural-constitutional Word, a polity-canon.

Farther into the vast realm of ecclesiology we shall not now proceed. For our aim here is simply to make available a hermeneutical tool, to develop the conceptual apparatus of canon and covenant in the hope that it might prove a useful instrument for the discovery of biblical answers to those questions about the form and function of the church that are being raised anew in our day.

Conclusion

Only in the Scriptures of the Old and New Testaments does the church possess infallible norms of faith and conduct. But though all the faith-norms of Scripture are, of course, permanent, not all the norms of conduct, or life-norms, found in Scripture are currently normative. When it comes to distinguishing among the life-norms those which have been abrogated from those which are still normative, the core of the problem centers in the relation of the life-norms of the Old Testament to the life of the church.

Analysis of the data may be clarified by approaching the matter with an historically and legally more precise concept of canon. If the covenantal concept of canon is utilized, in which the nuclear or definitive aspect of canonicity is discovered in the area of community polity, the basic relevant distinction that emerges is the distinction between individual life-norms and covenant community life-norms. It is the community life-norms, or polities, that are subject to abrogation as the covenant order undergoes major change.

In the customary affirmation of a single canon of Scripture which prescribes radically variant community polities for the people of God there is an obvious formal tension, which lures the theologian into scholastic or dialectical explanations of various sorts. This traditional tension is resolved by the recovery of the historically authentic concept of covenantal canon with its identification of the two treaty canons, old and new, within the church's Scriptures.

PART TWO

COLLATERAL STUDIES

Chapter One

THE TWO TABLES OF
THE COVENANT

"And he declared unto you his covenant, which he commanded you to perform, even ten commandments; and he wrote them upon two tables of stone" (Deut. 4:13).

It has been commonly assumed that each of the stone tables contained but a part of the total revelation proclaimed by the voice of God out of the fiery theophany on Sinai. Only the subordinate question of the dividing point between the "first" and "second tables" has occasioned disagreement.[1] A reexamination of the biblical data, however, particularly in the light of extrabiblical parallels, suggests a radically new interpretation of the formal nature of the two stone tables, the importance of which will be found to lie primarily in the fresh perspective it lends to our understanding of the divine oracle engraved upon them.

[1] The dominant opinion has been that the "second table" opens with the fifth commandment, but Jews usually count the fifth commandment as the last in the "first table," filial reverence being regarded as a religious duty. (Here and elsewhere in this chapter the designation of specific commandments is based on the common Protestant enumeration.) For a different ancient Jewish opinion anticipating the conclusion of the present study, see *Midrash Rabbah*, XLVII, 6.

Attention in recent years is being directed more and more to the remarkable resemblance between God's covenant with Israel and the suzerainty (also called vassal) type of international treaty found in the ancient Near East.[2] Similarities have been discovered in the areas of the documents, the ceremonies of ratification, the modes of administration, and, most basically, of course, the suzerain-servant relationship itself. On the biblical side, the resemblance is most apparent in the accounts of the theocratic covenant as instituted through the mediatorship of Moses at Sinai and as later renewed under both Moses and Joshua. Of most interest for the subject of this chapter is the fact that the pattern of the suzerainty treaty can be traced in miniature in the revelation written on the two tables by the finger of God.

"I am the Lord thy God," the opening words of the Sinaitic proclamation (Exod. 20:2a), correspond to the preamble of the suzerainty treaties, which identified the suzerain or "great king" and that in terms calculated to inspire awe and fear. For example, the treaty of Mursilis and his vassal Duppi-Teshub of Amurru begins: "These are the words of the Sun Mursilis, the great king, the king

[2] See G. E. Mendenhall, "Covenant Forms in Israelite Tradition," *The Biblical Archaeologist,* XVII, 3 (1954), 50-76; this was republished in *Law and Covenant in Israel and the Ancient Near East* (Pittsburgh, 1955). D. J. Wiseman had previously read a paper on some of the parallels to the Society for Old Testament Studies (Jan. 1948). Cf. K. Baltzer, *Das Bundesformular. Seine Ursprung und seine Verwendung im AT* (Wiss. Monogr. 2. A. und N.T., 4; Neukirchen, 1960).

There are references to such international treaties in the third millennium B.C. Actual treaty texts of the New Hittite Empire in the full classic form of the mid-second millennium B.C. were discovered some fifty years ago in the archives of ancient Hattusa. The evidence for this period has been supplemented by a few treaty fragments found at Ugarit. Other recent finds bring the evidence for vassal treaties down into the first half of the first millennium B.C. Most significant are the three Aramaic inscriptions from Sefireh and the Assyrian treaties of Esarhaddon found at Nimrud.

of the Hatti land, the valiant, the favorite of the Storm-god, the son of Suppiluliumas, etc."[3]

Such treaties continued in an "I-thou" style with an historical prologue surveying the great king's previous relations with, and especially his benefactions to, the vassal king. In the treaty just referred to, Mursilis reminds Duppi-Teshub of the vassal status of his father and grandfather, of their loyalty and enjoyment of Mursilis' just oversight, and climactically it is narrated how Mursilis, true to his promise to Duppi-Teshub's father, secured the dynastic succession for Duppi-Teshub, sick and ailing though he was. In the Decalogue the historical prologue is found in the further words of the Lord: "which have brought thee out of the land of Egypt, out of the house of bondage" (Exod. 20:2b). This element in the covenant document was clearly designed to inspire confidence and gratitude in the vassal and thereby dispose him to attend to the covenant obligations, which constitute the third element in both Exodus 20 and the international treaties.

There are many interesting parallels to specific biblical requirements among the treaty stipulations; but, to mention only the most prominent, the fundamental demand is always for thorough commitment to the suzerain to the exclusion of all alien alliances.[4] Thus, Mursilis insists: "But you, Duppi-Tessub, remain loyal toward the king of the Hatti land, the Hatti land, my sons (and) my grandsons forever. . . . Do not turn your eyes to anyone else!"[5] And Yahweh commands his servant: "Thou shalt have no other gods before me" (Exod. 20:3; cf. vv. 4, 5).

Stylistically, the apodictic form of the Decalogue apparently finds its only parallel in the treaties, which

[3] Translation of A. Goetze in *ANET*, p. 203. Cf. V. Korošec, *Hethitische Staatsverträge*, pp. 36ff.

[4] Cf. Korošec, *op. cit.*, pp. 66ff.; D. J. Wiseman, *The Vassal-Treaties of Esarhaddon* (London, 1958), pp. 23ff.; Mendenhall, *op. cit.*, p. 59.

[5] *ANET*, p. 204.

contain categorical imperatives and prohibitions and a conditional type of formulation equivalent to the apodictic curse (cf. Deut. 27:15-26), both being directly oriented to covenant oaths and sanctions. The legislation in the extant legal "codes," on the other hand, is uniformly of the casuistic type.

Two other standard features of the classic suzerainty treaty were the invocation of the gods of the suzerain and (in the Hittite sphere) the gods of the vassal as witnesses of the oath and the pronouncing of imprecations and benedictions, which the oath deities were to execute according to the vassal's deserts.

Obviously, in the case of God's covenant with Israel there could be no thought of a realistic invocation of a third party as divine witness.[6] Indeed, it is implicit in the third word of the Decalogue that all Israel's oaths must be sworn by the name of Yahweh (Exod. 20:7). The immediate contextual application of this commandment is that the Israelite must remain true to the oath he was about to take at Sinai in accordance with the standard procedure in ceremonies of covenant ratification (cf. Exod. 24).

Mendenhall[7] finds no reference to an oath as the foundation of the Sinaitic covenant; he does, however, allow that the oath may have taken the form of a symbolic act rather than a verbal formula. But surely a solemn affirmation of consecration to God made in the presence of God to his mediator-representative and in response to divine demand, sanctioned by divine threats against the rebellious, is tantamount to an oath. Moreover, Israel's eating and drinking in the persons of her

[6] There is a formal literary approximation to the invocation of the oath witnesses in Deuteronomy 4:26; 30:19; and 31:28, where, by the rhetorical device of apostrophe, God calls heaven and earth to be witnesses of his covenant with Israel. Heaven and earth are also invoked along with the mountains and rivers, etc., at the close of this section in the treaties. Cf. Matt. 5:34, 35; 23:16-22.

[7] *Op. cit.*, p. 66.

representatives on the mount of God (Exod. 24:11) was a recognized symbolic method by which people swore treaties.[8]

The curses and blessings are present in Exodus 20, though not as a separate section. They are, rather, interspersed among the stipulations (see vv. 5, 6, 7, 11, and 12). Moreover, an adaptation of the customary form of the curses and blessings to the divine nature of the Suzerain who here pronounced them was necessary. Thus, the usual invocative form has yielded to the declarative, and that in the style of the motive clause, which is characteristic of Old Testament legislation and illustrative of what may be called the reasonableness of Israel's Lord.[9]

There is one final point of material correspondence between Exodus 20 and the secular treaties. It provides the key to the nature of the two tables of stone, and to this we shall presently return. The parallelism already noted, however, is sufficient to demonstrate that the revelation committed to the two tables was rather a suzerainty treaty or covenant than a legal code. The customary exclusive use of "Decalogue" to designate this revelation, biblical terminology though it is (cf. "the ten words,"[10] Exod. 34:28; Deut. 4:13, 10:4), has unfortunately served to obscure the whole truth of the matter. That this designation is intended as only *pars pro toto* is

---

[8] Cf. Wiseman, *op. cit.*, p. 84, and lines 154-156 of the Ramataia text.

[9] Cf. B. Gemser, "The Importance of the Motive-Clause in Old Testament Law," *International Organization of Old Testament Scholars, Congress Volume, Copenhagen, 1953: Supplements to Vetus Testamentum*, I (Leiden, 1953), 50-66. It must be borne in mind that the Decalogue does not stand alone as the total revelation of the covenant at Sinai. For curses and blessings, see also the conclusion of the Book of the Covenant (Exod. 23:20-33); and cf. Deuteronomy 27-30.

[10] The contents of the treaties are also called the "words" of the suzerain.

confirmed by the fact that "covenant" ($b^e r \hat{\imath} t$; Deut. 4:13) and "the words of the covenant" (Exod. 34:28) are alternate biblical terminology. So, too, is "testimony" ($\bar{e} d \hat{u} t$; Exod. 25:16, 21; 40:20; cf. 2 Kings 17:15), which characterizes the stipulations as oath-bound obligations or as a covenant order of life.[11] Consequently, the two tables are called "the tables of the covenant" (Deut. 9:9, 11, 15) and "the tables of the testimony" (Exod. 31:18; 32:15; 34:29); the ark, as the depository of the tables, "the ark of the covenant" or "the ark of the testimony"; and the tabernacle, where the ark was located, "the tabernacle of the testimony."

The two stone tables are not, therefore, to be likened to a stele containing one of the half-dozen or so known legal "codes" earlier than or roughly contemporary with Moses, as though God had engraved on these tables a corpus of law.[12] The revelation they contain is nothing

[11] $\bar{e} d \hat{u} t$ is related to the Akkadian $ad \bar{e}$, which is used as a general appellation for the contents of suzerainty treaties. Wiseman (op. cit., p. 81) defines $ad \bar{u}$ (sing.) as "a law or commandment solemnly imposed in the presence of divine witnesses by a suzerain upon an individual or people who have no option but acceptance of the terms. It implies a 'solemn charge or undertaking on oath' (according to the view of the suzerain or vassal)."

[12] There does appear to be some literary relationship between the legal "codes" and the suzerainty treaties. J. Muilenburg ("The Form and Structure of the Covenantal Formulations," *Vetus Testamentum*, IX, 4 (1959), 347ff.) classifies both under "the royal message." Hammurapi in his "code," which is still the most complete of the extant ancient Oriental "codes," introduces himself in the prologue with a recital of his incomparable qualifications for the promulgation of laws, then presents the laws, and in the epilogue pronounces curses and blessings on future kings as they ignore or honor his "code." The identity of the Decalogue with the suzerainty treaties over against such law "codes" is evidenced by features like the covenant terminology, the $ad \bar{e}$ character of the stipulations, the "I-thou" formulation, and the purpose of the whole as manifested in both the contents and the historical occasion, i.e., the establishment of a covenant relationship between two parties.

less than an epitome of the covenant granted by Yahweh, the sovereign Lord of heaven and earth, to his elect and redeemed servant, Israel.

Not law, but covenant—that must be affirmed when we are seeking a category comprehensive enough to do justice to this revelation in its totality. At the same time, the prominence of the stipulations, reflected in the fact that "the ten words" are the element used as *pars pro toto,* signalizes the centrality of law in this type of covenant. There is probably no clearer direction afforded the biblical theologian for defining with biblical emphasis the type of covenant God adopted to formalize his relationship to his people than that given in the covenant he gave Israel to perform, even "the ten commandments." Such a covenant is a declaration of God's lordship, consecrating a people to himself in a sovereignly dictated order of life.

But what, now, is the significance of the fact that the covenant was recorded not on one but on two stone tables?

Apart from the dubious symbolic propriety of bisecting a treaty for distribution over two separate documents, all the traditional suggestions as to how the division should be made are liable to the objection that they do violence to the formal and logical structure of this treaty. The results of the traditional type of cleavage are not two reasonably balanced sets of laws but one table containing almost all of three of the four treaty elements plus a part of the fourth, i.e., the stipulations, and a second table with only a fraction of the stipulations plus possibly a blessing formula. The preamble and historical prologue must be neither minimized nor ignored because of their brevity, for this is a covenant in miniature. In comparison with the full-scale version, the stipulations are proportionately as greatly reduced as are the preamble and the historical prologue. That would be even clearer if the additional strand of the curses and blessings were not interwoven with the commandments. Certainly, too, there was no physical necessity for distributing the material over two stones. One table of such a size that Moses could carry, and the ark contain, a pair of them, would offer no problem of spatial limitations to prevent engraving the entire text upon it, especially since the writing covered both obverse and reverse (Exod. 32:15). In fact, it seems unreasonable, judging from the appearance of comparable stone inscriptions from antiquity, to suppose that all the area of both sides of two tables would be devoted to so few words.

There is, moreover, the comparative evidence of the extrabiblical treaties. Covenants such as Exodus 20:2-17 has been shown to be are found written in their entirety on one table and, indeed, like the Sinaitic tables, on both its sides.[13] As a further detail in the parallelism of external appearance it is tempting to see in the sabbath sign presented in the midst of the ten words the equivalent of the suzerain's dynastic seal found in the midst of the obverse of the international treaty documents. [14] Since in the case of the Decalogue the suzerain is Yahweh, there will be no representation of him on his seal; but the sabbath is declared to be his "sign of the covenant" (Exod. 31:13-17). By means of his sabbath-keeping, the image-bearer of God images the pattern of that divine act of creation which proclaims God's absolute sovereignty over man, and thereby he pledges his covenant consecration to his Maker. The Creator has stamped on world history the sign of the sabbath as his seal of ownership and authority. That is precisely what the pictures on the dynastic seals symbolize and their captions claim in behalf of the treaty gods and their representative, the suzerain.

[13] Cf., e.g., Wiseman, *op. cit.*, plates I and IX.

[14] The closing paragraph of the Egyptian text of the parity treaty of Hattusilis III and Ramses II is a description of the seal, called "What is in the middle of the tablet of silver" (*ANET*, p. 201). For the Mitannian practice of placing the seal on the reverse, cf. D. J. Wiseman, *The Alalakh Tablets* (London, 1953), plates VII and VIII, texts 13 and 14.

These considerations point to the conclusion that each stone was complete in itself. The two tables were duplicate copies of the covenant. And the correctness of this interpretation is decisively confirmed by the fact that it was normal procedure in establishing suzerainty covenants to prepare duplicate copies of the treaty text.

Five of the six standard sections of the classic suzerainty treaty were mentioned above. The sixth section contained directions for the depositing of one copy of the treaty document in the sanctuary of the vassal and another in a sanctuary of the suzerain.[15] For example, the treaty made by Suppiluliuma with Mattiwaza states: "A duplicate of this tablet has been deposited before the Sun-goddess of Arinna. . . . In the Mitanni land (a duplicate) has been deposited before Tessub. . . . At regular *intervals* shall they read it in the presence of the king of the Mitanni land and in the presence of the sons of the Hurri country."[16] Enshrinement of the treaty before the gods was expressive of their role as witnesses and avengers of the oath. Even the vassal's gods were thereby enlisted in the foreign service of the suzerain.[17]

Similar instructions were given Moses at Sinai concerning the two tables. They were to be deposited in the ark, which in turn was to be placed in the tabernacle (Exod. 25:16, 21; 40:20; Deut. 10:2). Because Yahweh was at once Israel's covenant Suzerain and God of Israel and of Israel's oath, there was but one sanctuary for the depos-

[15] Cf. Korošec, *op. cit.*, pp. 100-101. On a stele from Ras Shamra an oath-taking ceremony is depicted with the two parties raising their hands over two copies of the treaty (*Ugaritica* III, plate VI).

[16] Translation of A. Goetze, *ANET*, p. 205. In various treaties the public reading requirement specifies from one to three times annually.

[17] Cf. 2 Kings 18:25 and the observations of M. Tsevat, "The Neo-Assyrian and Neo-Babylonian Vassal Oaths and the Prophet Ezekiel," *Journal of Biblical Literature*, LXXVIII, 3 (1959), 199.

iting of both treaty duplicates. The specified location of the documents as given in Hittite treaties can be rendered "under (the feet of)" the god, which would then correspond strikingly to the arrangements in the Israelite holy of holies (see Exod. 25:22).[18] The two tables themselves do not contain instructions concerning their deposition, for the legislation regarding the ark and sanctuary had not yet been given. The same is true of the Book of the Covenant (Exod. 20:22-23:33). However, it is significant that when such legislation was given after the ceremony of covenant ratification (Exod. 24), the ark was the first object described in detail and directions for depositing the two tables in it were included (Exod. 25:10-22).

As for the further custom of periodic public reading of treaty documents, the contents of the two tables were, of course, declared in the hearing of all Israel and the Book of the Covenant was read to the people as part of the ratification ceremony (Exod. 24:7); but the practice of periodic proclamation was first formulated some forty years later in the Book of Deuteronomy when God was renewing the covenant unto the second generation. When suzerainty covenants were renewed, new documents were prepared in which the stipulations were brought up to date. Deuteronomy is such a covenant renewal document; hence its repetition with modernizing modifications of the earlier legislation, as found, for example, in its treatment of the Decalogue (5:6-21) or of the Passover (16:5ff.; cf. Exod. 12:7, 46).[19] Another case in point is Deuteronomy's addition of this requirement for the regular public reading of the covenant law at the Feast of Tabernacles in the seventh year of release (31:9-13), a

[18] Cf. Korošec, op. cit., p. 100.

[19] Taking Pentateuchal history at its face value, we discover that the Book of Deuteronomy exhibits precisely the legal form which contemporary second-millennium-B.C. evidence indicates a suzerain would employ in his rule of a vassal nation like Israel at such an historical juncture. See further, Part II, Chapter 2.

requirement that became relevant and applicable with the arrival of the Israelites at the threshold of their inheritance in Canaan. The document which was to be brought forth and read was not one of the stone tablets but the "book of the law" which Moses wrote and had placed by the side of the ark (31:9, 26). However, even if "this book of the law" is identified with Deuteronomy alone, reading it would have included a reproclamation of the contents of the tables.

The relevance of the foregoing for higher critical conclusions concerning the Decalogue may be noted in passing. Along with a decreasing reluctance in negative critical studies to accept the Mosaic origin of the Decalogue, [20] the judgment continues that the present form of the Sinaitic Decalogue is an expansion of the original, which is then reduced to an abridged version of the ten words, without preamble, historical prologue, or curses and blessings, and often without even an abridged form of the second and fourth words. Similarly, even where there is no bias against the Bible's representations concerning its own origins, the supposition has gained currency that it was an abbreviated version of the Decalogue that was engraved on the stone tables. Such estimates of the contents of the Mosaic tables are clearly unsatisfactory, since the supposed abbreviated forms lack those very features which distinguish the tables as that which comparative study indicates was called for by the historical occasion, and biblical exegesis indicates the tables to be, not a brief ethical catechism, but copies of the Sinaitic covenant.

The purpose of Israel's copy of the covenant was that of a documentary witness (Deut. 31:26).[21] It was wit-

20 Cf. H. H. Rowley, "Moses and the Decalogue," *Bulletin of the John Rylands Library*, XXXIV (1951-52), 81ff.

21 Various types of covenant witnesses other than the divine witness are mentioned. Cf. the Song of Moses, which he had Israel memorize (Deut. 31:19, 22; 32:1ff.); the stones with the law written upon them erected on Ebal (Deut. 27:2ff.; Josh. 8:30-35);

ness to and against Israel, reminding of obligations sworn to and rebuking for obligations violated, declaring the hope of covenant beatitude and pronouncing the doom of the covenant curses. The public proclamation of it was designed to teach the fear of the Lord to all Israel, especially to the children (Deut. 31:13; cf. Ps. 78:5ff.).

The secular treaties and the biblical covenant share a perspective of family solidarity reflected in numerous references to the sons and grandsons of the vassal. In the political treaties, sworn commitment is in the terms: "we, our sons, and our grandsons"; and agreeably both curses and blessings are pronounced unto children's children. "Visiting the iniquity of the fathers upon the children unto the third and fourth generation of them that hate me" (Exod. 20:5b) is the biblical counterpart, defining the bounds of corporate responsibility in guilt under this covenant administration by the utmost limits of contemporaneity (described here by means of numerical climax, a popular device of Hebrew and Canaanite literature).

Both copies of the covenant were laid before Yahweh as God of the oath. But what was the purpose of Yahweh's own copy in his capacity as covenant Suzerain? In the case of the international treaties, the suzerain would naturally want to possess, preserve, and protect a sealed legal witness to the treaty. It would remind him of the vassal's *adē* for the purpose of enforcement and punishment; for, according to the religious theory which was the legal fiction lending sacred sanction to the treaty, he would be the actual avenger of the oath, the instrument of the oath deities. It would also remind him of his suzerain's role as the vassal's protector and of the various specific promises of assistance often contained in such treaties. He had not, however, like the vassal, taken a covenant oath. And human lords being what they are, he would have had considerably less interest in the benefits

and the stone witness of covenant renewal at Shechem (Josh. 24:26, 27).

he might bestow on the vassal than in the amount of annual tribute he was entitled to exact from him.

Such, *mutatis mutandis,* was the purpose of Yahweh's own stone table of covenant witness. However, even from the formal point of view there is here a remarkable shift in emphasis arising from the fact that God's suzerainty covenant was an administration of salvation. The form of the blessing suggests the unique emphasis—"showing mercy," and that not merely to the third and fourth generation of them that love him but, contrary to the balance observed in this respect in the curse and blessing formulae of the international treaties, "to a thousand generations" (Deut. 7:9). This much more abounding of grace is evidenced even in connection with the function of the stone tables as witnesses against Israel; for since the divine throne under which the tables were located was the place of atonement, the witness of the tables against Israel never ascended to Yahweh apart from the witness of the blood advocating mercy.

The divine Suzerain's condescension in his redemptive covenant at the time of its Abrahamic administration extended to the humiliation of swearing himself to covenant fidelity as Lord of the covenant and Fulfiller of the promises (Gen. 15). Mendenhall[22] mistakenly regards the Abrahamic covenant as completely different in kind from the Sinaitic, partly because of God's oath and partly because of an alleged absence of obligations imposed on Abraham. Actually, the total allegiance to his Lord demanded of Abraham (Gen. 12:1; 17:1) was precisely that fealty which the treaty stipulations were designed to secure.

Moreover, it is demonstrable that an oath on the part of the suzerain was not incompatible with the genius of the relationship governed by a suzerainty treaty. There is, for example, a treaty with a related deed from Alalakh, [23]

22 *Op. cit.,* p. 62.
23 Published by D. J. Wiseman in the *Journal of Cuneiform*

both concerned with one Abban, the vizier of Hattusa, and his bestowment of certain cities upon his political "servant," Iarimlim. The treaty states that Abban confirmed the gifts in perpetuity by a self-maledictory oath accompanied by the symbolism of slaughtering a sheep. It also stipulates that the territorial gift is forfeit if Iarimlim is disloyal to Abban. The text deeding Alalakh (part of Abban's gift) pronounces curses upon any who would alter Abban's purpose by hostilities against Iarimlim.

All of this corresponds perfectly to God's dealings with Abraham. The Lord covenanted territory to his servant Abraham as an everlasting possession (Gen. 12:1, 2; 13:14-17; 15:18) and did so by a self-maledictory oath symbolized by the slaying of animals (Gen. 15:9ff.). Moreover, it is clear that by rebellion against Yahweh's word, Abraham would forfeit the promise (Gen. 22:16, 17a; cf. Deut. 28, esp. vv. 63ff.). And finally, the Egyptians and Canaanites who would oppose this territorial grant were cursed (Gen. 12:3; 15:14, 16, 19-21).

God's oath is, therefore, in keeping with the suzerain-vassal relationship. The generic nature of God's covenants with his people remains first and last a declaration of divine lordship, a lordship which may be manifested in the execution of promises or threats. These covenants are sovereign administrations not of blessing exclusively but of curse and blessing according to the vassal's deserts. Since, however, the specifically soteric covenants are informed by the principle of God's sovereign grace, which infallibly effects his redemptive purposes in Christ, they are accompanied by divine guarantees assuring a realization of the blessing sanctions of the covenant.

Now, it would obviously be unsound methodology to give this special feature which belongs to the specifically redemptive covenant administrations a constitutive place when defining the covenant generically. Nevertheless, there is not the least incompatibility between divine guarantees of blessing such as God's oath to Abraham, guarantees which, without violating human responsibility, assure the elect vassals that in Christ they will receive that covenant righteousness which is the stipulated way to covenant beatitude, and the nature of suzerainty covenants as they are here defined in terms of divine lordship, enforced in a revelation of law consisting of stipulations and sanctions, both promissory and penal.

Considered in relation to the divine oath and promise, Yahweh's duplicate table of the covenant served a purpose analogous to that of the rainbow in his covenant with Noah (Gen. 9:13-16). Beholding this table, he remembered his oath to his servants and faithfully brought to pass the promised blessing. And in that day when the four and twenty heavenly elders worship him saying, "Thy wrath is come, and the time of the dead, that they should be judged, and that thou shouldest give reward unto thy servants the prophets, and to the saints, and them that fear thy name, small and great," then, appropriately, the temple of God in heaven being opened, there is seen in his temple the ark of his covenant, the depository of God's table of remembrance (Rev. 11:17-19).

There remains the question of the relevance of our interpretation of the duplicate tables of the covenant for the understanding of their law content. The increased emphasis on the covenantal context of the law underscores the essential continuity in the function of law in the Old and New Testaments. The Decalogue is not offered fallen man as a genuine soteric option but is presented to him as a guide to citizenship within the covenant by the Saviour-Lord, who of his mercy delivers out of the house of bondage into communion in the life of the covenant—a communion that eventuates in perfect conformity of life to the law of the covenant. To stress the covenantal "I-thou" nature of this law is to reaffirm the personal-religious character of biblical ethics, as well as to recognize that covenantal religion and its ethics are susceptible to communication in the form of structured truth. Yahweh describes the beneficiaries of his mercy as "them that love me and keep my commandments" (Exod. 20:6; cf. John 14:15).

Recognition of the completeness of each of the tables provides a corrective to the traditional view's obscuration of the covenantal-religious nature of the laws in "the second table." A hegemony of religion over ethics has, indeed, always been predicated on the basis of the priority in order and verbal quantity of the laws of "the first table," analyzed as duty or love to God, over the laws of "the second table," analyzed as duty or love to man. Nevertheless, this very division of the ten words into "two tables," with the category of "love to God" used as a means of separating one "table" from the other, is liable to the misunderstanding that the fulfilling of the demands of "the second table" is in some degree, if not wholly, independent of the principle of love for God.

Our Lord's familiar teaching about a "first and great commandment" and a "second like unto it" (Matt. 22:37-40; Mark 12:29-31) has figured prominently in the speculation about the contents of "the two tables."[24] It is, however, gratuitous to suppose that Jesus was epitomizing in turn a "first table" and a "second table" as traditionally conceived. [25] Furthermore, it must be seriously questioned whether Jesus' commandment to love God's image-bearer, ourselves and our neighbors alike, can properly be restricted after the dominant fashion to the fifth through the tenth laws. The nearest parallel in the Decalogue to the specific language of Jesus is found in the fourth law as it is formulated in Deuteronomy

[24] In the Westminster Confession of Faith, for example, it is the only proof text cited for distinguishing between the "tables" in terms of duty toward God and duty to man (ch. XIX, sec. II).

[25] There is no explicit reference to the two stone tables in the context, which is broadly concerned with the generality of Scriptural legislation. Jesus relates his two commandments to the totality of Old Testament revelation (Matt. 22:40).

(5:14): the sabbath is to be kept "that thy manservant and thy maidservant may rest as well as thou." And does man not best serve the eternal interests of himself and of his neighbor when he promotes obedience to the first three commandments? Is that not the ethical justification of the Great Commission?

Beyond all doubt, Jesus' "great commandment" must be the heart motive of man in the whole compass of his life. Restricting the principle of love of God to the sphere of worship would prejudice the comprehensiveness of God's absolute lordship, which is the foundation of the covenant order.

That loving God with heart, soul, mind, and strength is as relevant to the tenth commandment as it is to the first is evident from the fact that to violate the tenth commandment is to worship Mammon; and we cannot love and serve both God and Mammon. Or consider the tenth word from the viewpoint of the principle of stewardship, the corollary of the principle of God's covenant lordship. Property in the Israelite theocracy was held only in fief under the Lord who declared: "For the land is mine; for ye are strangers and sojourners with me" (Lev. 25:23b). Therefore, to covet the inheritance of one's neighbor was to covet what was God's [26] and so to betray want of love for him. The application of this law is universal, because not just Canaan but "the earth is the Lord's and the fullness thereof, the world and they that dwell therein" (Ps. 24:1).

The comprehensiveness of Jesus' "first and great commandment" is evident from the preamble and historical prologue of the covenant document. Being introductory to the whole body of stipulations which follow, they are manifestly intended to inculcate the proper motivation

[26] Considered in this light, there is an exact equivalent to the tenth commandment in a Hittite treaty where the suzerain charges the vassal: "Thou shalt not desire any territory of the land of Hatti" (cited by Mendenhall, "Ancient Oriental and Biblical Law," *The Biblical Archaeologist*, XVII, 2 [1954], 30).

for obedience not to three or four or five of the stipulations but to them all; and the motivation they inspire is that of love to the divine Redeemer. Why are we to love our neighbors? Because we love the God who loves them; and, according to the principle articulated in the sabbath commandment (Exod. 20:11), the imperative to love God is also a demand to be like him.

The two commandments of Jesus do not distinguish two separable areas of human life but two complementary aspects of human responsibility. Our Lord's perspective is one with that of the duplicate tables of the covenant, which comprehend the whole duty of man within the unity of his consecration to his covenant Lord.

DYNASTIC COVENANT

New winds are blowing on the bark of Deuteronomic studies. It has managed not to drift very far from its Josianic (seventh century B.C.) dock only because of the unusually stout cables of critical traditionalism which tie it there.[1] The fate of so much higher critical treasure rides with this vessel that the scholarly merchants have been understandably anxious about its moorings and timid about entrusting it to the gods of wind and wave— especially since the winds seem to be blowing in the general direction of the Mosaic port, whence (so some say) the merchants pirated the craft.

Over thirty years ago, Gerhard von Rad signaled the need for discovering the nature and meaning of the over-all form of Deuteronomy.[2] Attention had been paid to the individual *Gattungen,* whether parenesis, legal precept, or curse-and-blessing formula. But what was the structural coherence of the several parts within the

1 For a survey of the more recent recommendations for a pre-Josianic or post-Josianic dating, see C. R. North, "Pentateuchal Criticism," *The Old Testament and Modern Study* (ed. H. H. Rowley; Oxford, 1951), esp. pp. 49ff.

2 "Das formgeschichtliche Problem des Hexateuch," *Beiträge zur Wissenschaft vom Alten und Neuen Testament,* 4. Folge, Heft 26, 1938; reprinted in G. von Rad, *Gesammelte Studien zum Alten Testament* (Munich, 1958).

whole? In current discussions this question is of crucial significance because the problem of the unity of Deuteronomy is judged to be not stylistic but structural.[3] Higher criticism has sought to distinguish an original core of Deuteronomy from the alleged accretions. Wellhausen and others have limited this core to chapters 12-26, but because of the stylistic homogeneity, most would now expand this to chapters 5-26 and chapter 28. It is the remaining chapters that are thought to disturb the structural unity and are regarded as editorial appendages. A. C. Welch, who distinguishes a Deuteronomic code (beginning in ch. 12) and framework, finds confusion throughout, but deems the framework in particular to be so hopelessly disordered that he declares it misleading to speak of editing, since that would suggest that a degree of order had been introduced into the chaos![4]

It is, then, with this issue of the structural unity and integrity of Deuteronomy that the present investigation is concerned. The question resolves itself into one of literary genre and *Sitz im Leben*. We believe it can be shown that what Mendenhall tentatively suggested concerning biblical history and law in general is certainly true in the case of Deuteronomy: "the literary criticism of the past has been proceeding with completely inadequate form-critical presuppositions."[5] The position to be advocated here is that Deuteronomy is a covenant renewal document which in its total structure exhibits the classic legal form of the suzerainty treaties of the Mosaic age.[6]

[3] Cf. G. E. Wright, "Deuteronomy," *The Interpreter's Bible* (Nashville, 1953), II, 314-318.

[4] *Deuteronomy: The Framework to the Code* (Oxford, 1932), pp. 8ff.

[5] "Covenant Forms in Israelite Tradition," *The Biblical Archaeologist*, XVII, 3 (1954), 70, n. 45. Cf. C. H. Gordon's broad development of this theme in "New Horizons in Old Testament Literature," *Encounter*, XXI, 2 (1960), 131-160.

[6] The present essay thus elaborates the identification of Deuteronomy made above; see p. 122, n. 19. While the pattern of the

Our procedure will be to trace the parallelism from beginning to end, observing especially the integrity of those sections of Deuteronomy whose presence has posed problems for the unity of the book. In this survey only major blocks of material are considered, but these will be sufficient to determine the validity of the thesis.

It will be useful to have a simple outline of the matter before us:[7] (1) Preamble (1:1-5); (2) Historical Prologue (1:6-4:49); (3) Stipulations (5-26); (4) Curses and Blessings or Covenant Ratification (27-30); (5) Succession Arrangements or Covenant Continuity, including the invocation of witnesses and the directions for the deposition and public reading of the treaty (31-34).

To analyze Deuteronomy in terms of a documentary pattern is not incompatible with the obvious fact that the book, according to its own representations, consists almost entirely of a series of addresses. For the specific kind of document in view would be orally proclaimed to the vassals at the covenant ceremony. Stylistically, this is reflected in the characteristic "I-thou" form of the suzerainty treaties, which is itself a point of correspondence with Deuteronomy. Also indicative of the oral proclamation of the covenant text is the evidence for an act of response by the vassal during the covenant ritual. Such a response is, in fact, incorporated into the very text of

suzerainty treaty has been widely recognized in the Decalogue and in Joshua 24, there has been a strange lack of acknowledgment of all the obvious facts in the case of Deuteronomy. Unfortunately, too, the covenant described in Joshua 24 has been interpreted on the horizontal level of a confederation of the twelve tribes with one another in an amphictyonic alliance rather than vertically as a renewal of Yahweh's lordship over the long since established theocracy. The very parallelism of the Joshua 24 covenant with the secular suzerainty treaties, as well as its clear continuity with and its obvious presupposing of the earlier Mosaic covenants, contradicts the interpretation of this event as the founding of the twelve-tribe system in Israel.

7 For a descriptive account of the treaty pattern, see above, pp. 114ff.

Esarhaddon's Nimrud treaty, where it consists of a self-maledictory oath binding the vassal to the lord's stipulations, these being repeated in summary in the response.[8] Deuteronomy also mentions the Amen to be uttered by the Israelites in the course of their ceremony (Deut. 27:15-26; cf. 26:17, 18; 29:12; Exod. 24:7; Josh. 24:16-18, 21, 24).[9]

The treaty document was thus the text of the covenant ceremony, sometimes including the response of the vassal as well as the declarations of the suzerain. When, therefore, we identify Deuteronomy as a treaty text, we are also recognizing it as the ceremonial words of Moses. The customary conception of these Mosaic addresses as a freely ordered farewell must be so far modified as to recognize that their formal structure closely followed fixed ceremonial-legal traditions, though they are certainly no stereotyped liturgical recital nor the dispassionate product of an imperial chancellery.

It will be recognized that this approach has a degree of formal affinity with the views of von Rad. Noting the succession of parenesis based on historical recital (1-11), laws (12-26:15), covenant engagement (26:16-19), and blessings and curses (27ff.)—a combination found also in the Sinai pericope of Exodus 19-24—von Rad concluded that this pattern points to the course of a great cultic celebration, specifically an ancient covenant renewal festival at Shechem.[10] We have no sympathy for von Rad's failure to recognize the historicity of the covenant renewal presented in Deuteronomy as a particular ceremony conducted by Moses in Moab. Neither are we

[8] Lines 494-512; cf. D. J. Wiseman, *The Vassal-Treaties of Esarhaddon*, p. 26.

[9] Similar is the Hittite soldiers' Amen to the curses both spoken and symbolized when they were pledging their loyalty to the king of Hatti land. See *ANET*, pp. 353ff.

[10] Cf. *op. cit.*, and *Studies in Deuteronomy* (London, 1953; a translation of *Deuteronomium-Studien*, Göttingen, 1948), pp. 14f.

persuaded that there was a periodic cultic ceremony held at Shechem. However, von Rad's formal analysis of the literary structure of Deuteronomy, based on his association of it with an alleged covenant renewal ceremony, did approximate what we judge to be the truth of the matter as that is now illuminated by more recent studies of international treaties. In their light the answer to the problem of Deuteronomy's literary genre can be formulated more accurately and fully than was possible at the time of von Rad's studies.

Deuteronomy begins precisely as the ancient treaties began: "These are the words of. . . ."[11] The Jewish custom of using the opening words of a book as its title turns out in the present case to be most felicitous, for it serves to identify this book at once as a treaty document.[12] Deuteronomy 1:1-5 then goes on to identify the speaker of "the words" as Moses, one who receives divine revelation and communicates the sovereign will of the Lord to Israel. Yahweh is, therefore, the Suzerain who gives the covenant and Moses is his vicegerent and the covenant mediator. This section thus corresponds to the preamble of the extrabiblical treaties, which also identified the speaker, the one who was by the covenant declaring his lordship and claiming his vassal's allegiance.[13]

"A major problem concerning the unity of Deuteronomy has been the presence of the two introductions (chs. 1-4 and 5-11) to the legal section in chs. 12-26. Neither introduction needs the other; they seem to be indepen-

11 Wherever the beginning of a Hittite suzerainty treaty has been preserved, *umma*, the particle used for introducing direct discourse, is found. Compare, too, the Bible's familiar introductory formula: "Thus saith the Lord."

12 Altogether misleading, on the contrary, is the English title, which is apparently based on the Septuagint's mistranslation of the phrase, "a copy of this law" (17:18), as *to deuteronomion touto*, "this second law."

13 Cf. above, p. 114.

dent of each other." So states G. E. Wright,[14] and then adopts M. Noth's solution. This solution is bound up with the larger issue of Deuteronomy's relation to other canonical books. Noth,[15] like Engnell, would detach Deuteronomy from the Pentateuch and attach it to the Former Prophets, thus making it the beginning of and the philosophy for a Deuteronomic history that continues through 2 Kings. The opening chapters of Deuteronomy are, according to Noth, an introduction to this history as a whole. The Deuteronomic laws as such are thereby left with only one introduction, i.e., chapters 5 (or 4:44)-11.

But Noth's view (like every attempt to separate Deut. 1-4 from an original core) is contradicted, the supposed problem of the two introductions is obviated, and the real structure of Deuteronomy is further clarified by these facts: an historical prologue regularly follows the preamble and precedes the stipulations in the suzerainty treaties,[16] and Deuteronomy 1:5-4:49 admirably qualifies as such an historical prologue.[17] When covenants were renewed, the history was brought up to date. Agreeably, Moses takes up the narrative of Yahweh's previous rule over Israel at Horeb, where the theocratic covenant was originally made (though, as often elsewhere, he roots this development in the earlier Abrahamic covenant; cf. Deut. 1:8), and he carries the history up to the present, emphasizing the most recent events, the Transjordanian conquests and their consequences.

Deuteronomy 4 is noteworthy in that it exhibits, at least to a degree, each of the constitutive features of the

[14] *Op. cit.*, p. 316, n. 13.

[15] M. Noth, *Ueberlieferungsgeschichtliche Studien* I (Halle, 1943).

[16] Cf. above, p. 115.

[17] Deuteronomy 4:44-49 may be assigned to the historical prologue or to the stipulations that follow; it provides a summarizing conclusion for the one and an introduction to the other and is thus transitional.

treaty pattern: the identification of the speaker (vv. 1, 2, 5, 10); the appeal to covenant history (vv. 10ff., 20ff., etc.); the basic stipulation of undivided allegiance (vv. 15ff., etc.); the blessing-curse sanctions (vv. 27ff.); the invocation of witnesses (v. 26); and the arrangements for the perpetuation of the covenant (vv. 9, 10, 21, 22). This reflection of the total treaty pattern within the undisputed unity of this brief passage is a significant clue to the nature of the larger document in which it is embedded and is an interesting indication of how Moses' thought and expression this day were operating within the traditional forms required by the occasion. In his mind he sees the whole course of the ceremony with its call for decision and solemn sanctions, and in the urgency of these his final words to the people whom he has so long served he summarily anticipates all that is about to transpire.

The third division of suzerainty treaties was the stipulations,[18] and this division of Deuteronomy can be readily identified with chapters 5-26. Von Rad, as noted above, included chapters 5-11 with chapters 1-4 as a sermonic historical survey. Others, separating chapters 5-11 from chapters 1-4, regard the former as an introduction to chapters 12-26. But Deuteronomy 5-11 must be recognized as expounding the covenant way of life, just as do chapters 12-26. Together they declare the Suzerain's demands. The differences between Deuteronomy 5-11 and 12-26 merely represent differing treatments of this one theme. The former section presents in more general and comprehensive terms the primary demand of consecration to the Lord, both as principle (ch. 6) and as program (ch. 7); the latter adds the more specific, ancillary requirements. Of particular interest is the fact that this sequence from the fundamental to the auxiliary commandments corresponds to the arrangement of the stipulations observable in extrabiblical treaties. They first

18 Cf. above, pp. 115f.

formulate the basic demand for tributary allegiance, then proceed to the details of military cooperation, extradition, etc.[19]

One cannot help but notice also how the programmatic mandate of conquest (Deut. 7), which implements the call for perfect loyalty to Yahweh by its demand for the obliteration of rival gods with their cults and devotees within Yahweh's chosen holy domain, corresponds to the military clauses in the treaties. Another interesting parallel is found in the Deuteronomic version of the customary stipulation forbidding the vassal to pay tribute to any but the covenant suzerain. This is noteworthy in connection with a denial of the integrity of Deuteronomy 12:1-7 like that of Welch. For it is this authentic treaty motif that clearly provides the rationale of the reformulation of the earlier law concerning the central altar in Deuteronomy 12 and constitutes the underlying unity of all the precepts, permissions, and prohibitions in that chapter.

The hortatory character of the Deuteronomic stipulations, even of those in chapters 12-26, exposes the inaccuracy of speaking of a Deuteronomic law code. But this feature is not without parallel in the formulation of the treaty stipulations. We are reminded of Moses' recalling the lessons of Israel's past history when we find Mursilis enforcing his demand for three hundred shekels of gold by exhorting Duppi-Teshub: "Do not turn your eyes to anyone else! Your fathers presented tribute to Egypt; you [shall not do that]!"[20] This documentary feature would naturally be fully exploited by Moses when conducting the renewal ceremony that was also his personal farewell, and as impressive an occasion as ever challenged

[19] See the treaty between Mursilis and Duppi-Teshub in *ANET*, pp. 203-204, where the primary stipulation is separately paragraphed as "Future Relations of the Two Countries." A similar sequence is found in parity treaties; cf. *ibid.*, pp. 199-203.

[20] Translation of A. Goetze, *ANET*, p. 204.

an orator. It is, therefore, a quite unnecessary and misguided effort when von Rad seeks to account for the
interspersion of the commandments with parenesis in
terms of later Levitical preaching of the law at a cultic
festival.[21]

One further point of correspondence to the treaties
may be mentioned in connection with the stipulations.
Deuteronomy's repetition of the Decalogue and of other
earlier legislation, with such modifications as were required by Israel's imminent change of environment from
desert to city and sown, accords with the suzerains'
practice of repeating but modernizing their demands
when they renewed covenants.[22]

In the covenant ceremony the vassal took his oath in
response to the stipulations and under the sanctions of
the curses and blessings, which are found as the fourth
standard section in the treaties.[23] This decisive act in
Israel's ceremony in Moab is reflected at the conclusion
of the Deuteronomic stipulations (Deut. 26:17-19; cf.
Exod. 24:7) and within the Deuteronomic curse-blessing
section (Deut. 27-30, esp. 29:10-15; cf. 27:15-26). This
element of promissory and penal sanctions that chapters
27-30 have in common, finding as it does its counterpart
in content, context, and function in the extrabiblical
covenant documents, evidences the unity of these chapters and their integrity within the total original Deuteronomic document. The usual scholarly conclusion that
chapter 28 belongs with chapters 12-26, while chapters
27, 29, and 30 are unoriginal appendixes of unknown but
late date, betrays a lack of appreciation for the relevant
form-critical data.[24] The fact that the curse-blessing

21 Cf. *Studies in Deuteronomy,* pp. 13ff.

22 Cf. above, pp. 122f.

23 Cf. above, pp. 116f.

24 Cf. G. E. Wright's remark: "Again the difficulty is largely
structural" (*op. cit.,* p. 317). Naturalistic stumbling over the pre-
view of Israel's distant exile and restoration contained in these

motif in Deuteronomy 27 takes the form of directions
for a subsequent ceremony to be conducted by Joshua at
Shechem has lent itself to the dissociation of this chapter from its context. However, as will be shown below, if
Deuteronomy's own account of its historical origin is
respected and the significance of the theme of dynastic
succession is properly appraised, the integrity of Deuteronomy 27 becomes apparent.

In this section, as in Deuteronomy 4, an accumulation
of the major treaty elements is found within short compass, forming a concentrated covenant pattern as the
framework for the great call for decision (Deut.
30:15-20). There is historical recital of the Lord's mighty
acts of grace (Deut. 29:2ff.); a reiteration of the primary
stipulation to love God, with the corollary prohibition of
alien alliances (Deut. 29:18ff.); the invocation of heaven
and earth as witnesses (Deut. 30:19); and, of course, the
curses and blessings throughout chapters 27-30.

Worthy of parenthetical comment is the fact that the
Mosaic curses and blessings provided the outline for the
eschatological message of the prophets. In the nature of
the case, the blessings and curses of a covenant whose
lord was Yahweh, sovereign Judge of history, could not
but be prophecy. If it had been earlier recognized that
the common roots of prophetic woe and weal are located
here in the sanctions of Israel's ancient covenant, the
tendency of literary criticism to distinguish sharply between the provenance of the weal and woe strands in the
writings of the prophets might have been forestalled.
Awareness of this unity of antonymic sanctions within
the *literary* tradition of covenant documents should also
serve to dampen the more recent enthusiasm for tracing
the judgment-restoration theme of the prophets to a
hypothetical Israelite cultic drama of disaster and deliverance.[25]

chapters has certainly contributed more to the dominant higher
critical dating of them than have the alleged structural difficulties.

[25] Cf. F. C. Fensham, "Malediction and Benediction in Ancient

The closing chapters (Deut. 31-34) have been generally dismissed as miscellaneous appendixes. If, however, one looks beyond the surface fact that there is a variety of literary forms in these chapters and takes his analytical cue from the treaty pattern observed hitherto in the book, he is bound to come to quite another conclusion. For Deuteronomy 31-34 is consistently concerned with the continuity and perpetuation of the covenant relationship, and all the elements in this section serve to corroborate the identification of Deuteronomy in its entirety as an integral suzerainty treaty.

Included here are the final two standard elements in the classic treaty structure. One is the enlisting of witnesses to the covenant. Heaven and earth are again summoned to this office (Deut. 31:28; 32:1; cf. 4:26; 30:19); but most prominent is the Song of Witness (31:16-22; 31:28-32:45), which is to be in Israel's own mouth as God's witness against them in the days to come (31:19).[26] The other customary feature is the direction for the depositing of the treaty text in the sanctuary and for its periodic reproclamation (31:9-13).[27] This arrangement, while it served the end of perpetuating the covenant in that it was a means for the inspirational instruction of successive generations in the words of God's law (31:12, 13; 32:46), was yet another witness to the covenant (31:26).

For the rest, the closing chapters are concerned in one way or another with the Moses-Joshua succession. This succession was appointive and charismatic, not genealogical; but insofar as these men were mediators between God and Israel, and thus successive representatives of the

Near Eastern Vassal-Treaties and the Old Testament," *Zeitschrift für die Alttestamentliche Wissenschaft,* LXXIV, 1 (1962), 1-9.

[26] Cf. above, pp. 116f. On the literary form of the Song of Witness in Deuteronomy 32, see the valuable article by J. Harvey, "Le 'RIB-Pattern,' réquisitoire prophétique sur la rupture de l'alliance," *Biblica,* XLIII, 2 (1962), 172-196.

[27] Cf. above, pp. 121ff.

unchanging rule of Yahweh over Israel, their succession may be designated dynastic. There was, indeed, a peculiar unity between Moses and Joshua. The earlier intimate association of Joshua with Moses in the latter's mediatorial prerogatives on the Sinaitic mount of theophany suggests a kind of identification—a "dynastic" oneness of the two. Moreover, the work accomplished through the two was one redemptive complex, the one great Old Testament salvation, consisting in deliverance from Egypt and inheritance of Canaan. It was Moses' anticipation that he should complete this work himself, but unexpectedly he was disqualified and was obliged to ascend the mount to die. Joshua, however, might be thought of as a Moses *redivivus*. Continuing in the spirit and power of Moses, he completes the soteric drama begun under Moses. Joshua perfects the typological unit: out of bondage into paradise land. It is, of course, only in terms of such human mediatorial representatives that dynastic succession is predicable of the rule of the King eternal, immortal, invisible. But at that level there does exist a theocratic analogy to dynastic succession in human kingdoms.

This subject of the royal succession clearly contributes to the motif of covenant continuity and, hence, enhances the thematic coherence of Deuteronomy 31-34. It is also a further mark of Deuteronomy's literary identity. For the throne succession of the suzerain's house figures very prominently in the suzerainty treaties.[28] In fact, the vassal's oath of allegiance was directed to both the suzerain and his successors. The most significant available evidence on this point is the Nimrud treaty of Esarhaddon, for it is occupied exclusively with this one subject of royal succession.[29] It is the text of the covenant ceremony at which Esarhaddon's vassals were required to

[28] Cf. V. Korošec, *Hethitische Staatsverträge*, pp. 66-67; cf. pp. 63f.

[29] See D. J. Wiseman, *op. cit.*, p. 28.

acknowledge by oath the succession rights of Ashurbanipal as crown prince of Assyria and of his brother,
Shamash-shum-ukin, as crown prince of Babylonia.[30]

In this connection there comes into focus the two-
stage nature of Yahweh's ceremonial renewal of his covenant with Israel. The ceremony insuring Ashurbanipal's
throne-rights was held, as it turned out, just four years
before the elderly Esarhaddon's death. Then, as was customary, soon after the accession of Ashurbanipal there
was another ceremony for the confirmation of the vassals' fealty to him.[31] Such, we take it, is the relationship
of the covenant ceremony conducted by Moses in Moab
and documented in the Book of Deuteronomy to the
covenant ceremony conducted by Joshua at Mount Ebal
and Mount Gerizim and reported in Joshua 8:30-35. The
first stage takes place when the death of Moses, the
Lord's representative, is imminent.[32] Yahweh's continuing lordship is reaffirmed in a ceremony in which his
appointment of Joshua to be Moses' successor as vicegerent is announced (Deut. 31:3) and Joshua is divinely
commissioned (Deut. 31:14, 23; cf. 31:7ff.). Accordingly, Israel's renewed oath of obedience to the Lord em-
braces a commitment to follow Joshua (cf. Deut. 34:9;
Josh. 1:16-18), that is, to submit to Yahweh's expressed

[30] Legal provision is also made in the treaties with respect to
the dynastic succession within the vassal kingdom. So, for example,
Suppiluliuma stipulates that the Mitannian throne succession shall
go to the offspring of the marriage of the vassal, Mattiwaza, and
the daughter of Suppiluliuma (cf. Korošec, op. cit., p. 70). This
concern with vassal dynasty might also offer a counterpart to the
Moses-Joshua succession in Deuteronomy, for the dual character of
their mediatorial role meant that they were not only God's vicegerents over Israel but Israel's representatives before God and thus a
charismatic "dynasty" of vassal kings.

[31] Cf. Wiseman, op. cit., pp. 3ff.

[32] If Moses and Joshua were being viewed as vassal kings, the
timing of the covenant renewal could be related to the practice of
renewing suzerainty treaties when death occasioned a change of
vassal rulers.

will regarding the dynastic succession. The second stage of the ceremony was held at Shechem not long after Moses' death and Joshua's accession, when the Lord had attested his presence with Joshua as with Moses by duplicating the Mosaic signs of victory over the waters and hostile hosts. There Israel was summoned to confirm its consecration to the Lord according to all the words in the Mosaic book of the law and, hence, to confirm its recognition of Joshua as representative of God's appointment in succession to Moses.

Far from being appendant fragments worked in by an editorial eclectic, the dynastic succession material in Deuteronomy 31-34 treats of that which was the very occasion for the covenant renewal and thus for the whole Book of Deuteronomy. Joshua's succession was the most prominent symbol of Yahweh's continuing theocratic lordship and, therefore, it was of fundamental and supreme significance in the covenant ceremony and document.[33] By the same token, the Shechem ceremony, as the cultic confirmation of Joshua's succession, emerges as the climactic act in the process of covenant renewal. This explains the appearance of the directions for this final ratification (Deut. 27) at the structural climax of the book, following the stipulations and at the beginning of the section on curses and blessings or covenant ratification. We have placed Deuteronomy 27 in the latter division, but it is to be observed that the form is that of commandment and it might well be included with the stipulations. In either case the directions for the covenant ritual on Mount Ebal and Mount Gerizim constitute the central demand and goal of the Deuteronomic treaty. Here is the heart of the whole matter and that is why it appears at the heart of the book.[34]

[33] Noteworthy is Moses' preoccupation with this theme, manifested by its recurrence at pivotal points even in the earlier chapters (Deut. 3:21ff.; 11:29-32; cf. Deut. 1:38).

[34] It is always easier to criticize ancient texts than it is to understand them, and here again a facile higher criticism has

It may be observed in passing that Deuteronomy's interest in the perpetuity of Yahweh's rule and specifically its concern with the security of the dynastic succession of Yahweh's vicegerents in Israel is a mark of the profound unity between the Deuteronomic and the Davidic covenants. Mendenhall believes that there is a fundamental tension between these covenants, the same tension which, as was noted earlier, he finds between the Mosaic and the Abrahamic covenants.[35] Commenting on the discovery of Deuteronomy in Josiah's day, Mendenhall says that "what was rediscovered was not old legislation, but the basic nature of the old amphictyonic covenant. It brought home to Josiah and the religious leadership that they had been living in a fool's paradise in their assumption that Yahweh had irrevocably committed Himself to preserve the nation in the Davidic-Abrahamic covenant. Moses was rediscovered."[36] The resolution of

followed the path of least resistance by condemning Deuteronomy 27 as structurally disruptive, a break in the connection between chapters 26 and 28, and certainly "not originally intended for this place" (cf. Wright, *op. cit.,* p. 488). Critics of the prevalent theory that Deuteronomy was designed to promote the centralization of the cultus in Jerusalem have pointed to the awkwardness of Deuteronomy's references to Shechem as a cultic site. In order to maintain even a modified version of that theory in the face of such criticism, H. H. Rowley has been obliged to attribute to the supposed late compilers a remarkable degree of political vision and of immunity to religious provincialism and prejudice (see his "The Prophet Jeremiah and the Book of Deuteronomy," *Studies in Old Testament Prophecy* [ed. H. H. Rowley; New York, 1950], pp. 165-167). The untenability of his defense must become the more evident should he attempt to account not merely for the presence but the climactic import of Joshua's Shechemite ceremony within the Deuteronomic treaty.

[35] See above, p. 125. J. Bright, in his *A History of Israel* (Philadelphia, 1959), pp. 203ff., 300, follows Mendenhall in this misconception, working it out in so thoroughgoing a fashion in his reconstruction of the monarchy that it assumes the proportions of a major flaw in his work.

[36] *The Biblical Archaeologist,* XVII, 3 (1954), 73.

this alleged tension was eventually provided, Mendenhall suggests, in the new covenant concept through its emphasis on divine forgiveness.

It would seem that a want of theological perspicacity is to blame, at least in part, for Mendenhall's mistranslation of the biblical history into this quite fictional version. For what he interprets as conflict between covenants is in the last analysis simply the fundamental theological paradox of divine sovereignty and human responsibility that confronts us in all divine-human relationships. Mendenhall has separated the two members of this paradox, both of which are inevitably present in every administration of God's covenants with man, and has arbitrarily assigned one side of the paradox to the Mosaic covenant and the other to the Abrahamic-Davidic covenants.

Now in the redemptive covenants that are under discussion, the divine sovereignty comes to sharpest focus in the promises of blessing to which absolute guarantees are attached, while human responsibility is presupposed in the covenant stipulations, pointedly so in the accompanying threats of curse. Both of these elements are present in the Davidic covenant. For along with its dynastic guarantee, responsibility and judgment are announced (2 Sam. 7:14). Nor, on the other hand, is the aspect of guaranteed blessing absent from the Deuteronomic covenant. In fact, it too contains a divine oath sealing God's promise of redemptive judgment (Deut. 32:40). And elsewhere in this treaty Moses proclaims the certainty of the covenant-renewing grace of God, by which his oath-sealed promise to the fathers would be fulfilled to the elect in spite of Israel's covenant-breaking and the visitation of the full vengeance of the covenant upon the guilty (Deut. 4:29-31; 30:1-10; cf. Lev. 26:40-45). Not for the first time at some later stage in Old Testament revelation but here in the Mosaic foundation of the Old Testament canon the prospect of the new covenant emerges. Moreover, in the divine-human mediator of this new covenant there is a manifestation of the unity of the Deuteronomic and the Davidic covenants. For it is in him that the promise inherent in the royal commission given to the Moses-Joshua dynasty to lead the people of God into their rest is truly fulfilled, just as it is in him and his royal session at the right hand of the Majesty on high that the Davidic dynasty has, according to the divine promise, been established forever.

We are also in a position now to appreciate the fact that the record of Moses' death and of his testamentary blessings on the tribes (Deut. 33, 34) belongs to the original Deuteronomic document. To refer again to Esarhaddon's Nimrud treaty, the essence of it is expressed in the following statement: "*When Esarhaddon, king of Assyria, dies,* you will seat Ashurbanipal, the crown prince, upon the royal throne, he will exercise the kingship (and) lordship of Assyria over you."[37] The dynastic succession stipulation—in effect, the whole covenant since it was concerned solely with dynastic succession—became of force at the death of Esarhaddon. It was the death of the covenant's author that caused the covenant stipulations and sanctions to become operative. That, we would suggest, is the legal key to the understanding of the structural integrity of Deuteronomy 33 and 34 within the context of the whole document. When Moses, Yahweh's mediator-king of Israel, died, an official affixed to the Deuteronomic treaty the notice of that death,[38] so validating the document, particularly as to its central concern, the enforcement of Yahweh's royal succession

[37] Translation by Wiseman, *op. cit.,* lines 46-49 (italics ours); cf. lines 188-191.

[38] This official could also have well been responsible for certain brief paragraphs which were not part of the covenant ceremony conducted by Moses but purely documentary formulations added to round out the treaty pattern, e.g., the preamble (Deut. 1:1-5) or a passage like Deuteronomy 4:44-49, which labels a treaty section. Cf. G. T. Manley, *The Book of the Law* (London, 1957), pp. 150-162.

and the continuance thereby of the lordship of heaven over Israel.

The inclusion in the covenant document of Moses' final blessings upon the tribes (Deut. 33) underscores an important legal datum, namely, the coalescence of the covenantal and the testamentary forms. From the viewpoint of the subject people, a treaty guaranteeing the suzerain's dynastic succession is an expression of their covenantal relation to their overlord; but from the viewpoint of the royal son(s) of the suzerain, the arrangement is testamentary. Testament and suzerainty-covenant are not simple equivalents, but to the extent that the latter is concerned with dynastic succession it is informed by the primary administrative principle of the testament: it is not in force while the testator lives.

From Joshua's point of view as heir appointive over Israel, the Book of Deuteronomy in its entirety was a Mosaic testament. But Deuteronomy 33 is a testament to which all Israel was beneficiary. This fact compels us to reckon with still another facet of the multiform religious relationship between Israel and Yahweh. Israel's divine election was unto adoption as well as unto the giving of the law (Rom. 9:4). The Israelites were, therefore, sons as well as servants (cf. Exod. 4:22; Deut. 14:1), and Moses as God's representative was unto them as father as well as king. Moreover, as sons of the heavenly King, they were all heirs to a royal reign. Indeed, the establishment of Israel as a royal priesthood over Canaan was in a figure a reinstatement of man as vicegerent of God over paradise. At the same time, though the concept of all God's people participating in Moses' gifts and functions comes to expression even in the Pentateuch (Num. 11:16ff., esp. v. 29; cf. Deut. 34:9), Israel the heir was under governors until the time appointed of the Father (Gal. 4:1, 2). The emphasis remained on servanthood rather than sonship until new covenant times (cf. Gal. 4:7; Rom. 8:17).

Several New Testament passages that deal expressly with covenant administration might be profitably re-examined in the light of the new evidence, particularly Hebrews 9:16, 17. The problem in that passage has been that it appears illogical to establish principles of covenantal administration by appealing to procedures that govern testamentary dispositions, since the two seem to be totally distinct legal forms. If, however, one assumes that the author's parenthetical allusion in these verses is to the dynastic-testamentary aspect of ancient suzerainty covenants and especially of the old covenant as exemplified by Deuteronomy, the way is open for a satisfactory solution. Hebrews is, of course, pervasively occupied with a comparison of the covenants mediated by Jesus and Moses. It is also significant that one of its recurrent themes is dynastic appointment and perpetuity (cf. Heb. 1:2ff., 8; 5:6ff.; 6:20ff.), the precise area of covenantal administration for which the merging of the covenantal and the testamentary is attested. If that is indeed the area of reference in Hebrews 9:16, 17, then the picture suggested is that of Christ's children (cf. 2:13) inheriting his universal dominion as their eternal portion (note 9:15b; cf. 1:14; 2:5ff.; 6:17; 11:7ff.). And such is the wonder of the Messianic mediator-testator that the royal inheritance of his sons, which becomes of force only through his death, is nevertheless one of co-regency with the living testator! For (to follow the typological direction provided by Heb. 9:16, 17 according to the present interpretation) Jesus is both dying Moses and succeeding Joshua. Not merely after a figure but in truth a royal mediator *redivivus,* he secures the divine dynasty by succeeding himself in resurrection power and ascension glory.

In the light of the evidence now surveyed, it would seem indisputable that the Book of Deuteronomy, not in the form of some imaginary original core but precisely in the integrity of its present form, the only one for which there is any objective evidence, exhibits the structure of the ancient suzerainty treaties in the unity and completeness of their classic pattern. That there should be a measure of oratorical and literary enrichment of the traditional legal form is natural, considering the caliber of the author and the grandeur of the occasion. And, of course, there is the conceptual adaptation inevitable in the adoption of common formal media for the expression of the unique revelation of God in the Scriptures. What is remarkable is the detailed extent to which God has utilized this legal instrument of human kingdoms for the definition and administration of his own redemptive reign over his people.

The implication of the new evidence for the questions of the antiquity and the authenticity of Deuteronomy must not be suppressed. The kind of document with which Deuteronomy has been identified did not originate in some recurring ritual situation. Treaties were, of course, prepared for particular historical occasions. In order, therefore, to account satisfactorily for the origin of the Deuteronomic treaty, it is necessary to seek for an appropriate historical episode in the national life of Israel. Without now rehearsing all the data that make it perfectly apparent that it was to the recently founded theocratic nation that the treaty was addressed, we would press only one question: Where, either in monarchic or premonarchic times, where except in the very occasion to which Deuteronomy traces itself can an historical situation be found in which the twelve tribes would have been summoned to a covenantal engagement whose peculiar purpose was, as the purpose of the Deuteronomic treaty demonstrably was, to guarantee the continuance of a (non-Davidic) dynasty over Israel?

Still another index of the time of Deuteronomy's composition is provided by the evolution of the documentary form of suzerainty treaties. Admittedly, the available evidence is still quite limited and the differences among the extant treaties are not to be exaggerated. It is indeed one species that we meet throughout Old Testament times. Nevertheless, there is a discernible evolution. [39]

[39] W. F. Albright asserts that the structure of the later treaties

For example, where the beginning is preserved in the first-millennium-B.C. treaties of Sefireh and Nimrud, it is not the opening *umma* of the second-millennium-B.C. treaties, or its equivalent. Also, in the Sefireh treaties only a trace remains of the blessing sanctions that are prominent in the earlier treaties, and the sanctions in Esarhaddon's treaties consist exclusively of curses. The most remarkable difference is that the historical prologue, the distinctive second section of the second-millennium treaties, is no longer found in the later texts.

Accordingly, while it is necessary to recognize a substantial continuity in pattern between the earlier and later treaties, it is proper to distinguish the Hittite treaties of the second millennium B.C. as the "classic" form. And without any doubt the Book of Deuteronomy belongs to the classic stage in this documentary evolution. Here, then, is significant confirmation of the prima facie case for the Mosaic origin of the Deuteronomic treaty of the Great King.

The literary genre of Deuteronomy also has important implications for the way in which this document, having once been produced, would have been transmitted to subsequent generations. By their very nature treaties like Deuteronomy were inviolable. They were sealed legal commitments. Indeed, as has already been observed, it was standard practice to deposit such treaties in sanctuaries under the eye of the oath deities.

Moreover, there are interesting examples in some of the extant texts of specific curses pronounced against anyone who would in any way violate the treaty inscriptions. Referring to the treaty tablet which bore the seal of Ashur, Esarhaddon declared: "(You swear that) you will not alter (it), you will not consign (it) to the fire nor

"is quite different" from the Syro-Anatolian treaties of the fourteenth-thirteenth centuries B.C.; *From the Stone Age to Christianity* (New York, 1957), p. 16. For a cautious statement of the case, see J. L'Hour, "L'Alliance de Sichem," *Revue Biblique*, LXIX, 1 (1962), 15.

throw (it) into the water, nor [bury (it)] in the earth nor destroy it by any cunning device, nor make [(it) disappear], nor sweep (it) away. (If you do,) [may Ashur, king of the] gods who decrees the fates, [decree for you] evil and not good."[40]

Similarly a special curse is included in the Sefireh I and II treaties against anyone responsible for effacing the inscriptions from their steles.[41] The sacredness of the treaty steles is enhanced in the curse of Sefireh II by designating them "the houses of the gods" (*bty 'lhy'*) or "bethels." [42]

Corresponding to these special stele curses is the injunction of Deuteronomy 4:2a, set in a context of covenant sanctions: "Ye shall not add unto the word which I

[40] Lines 410-415a; the translation is that of D. J. Wiseman, *op. cit.*, p. 60. Cf. lines 397ff. The description of the series of actions by which the tablet might be destroyed corresponds remarkably to the description of Moses' treatment of the stone tables of the covenant and of the golden calf in Exodus 32:19b, 20. It would seem clear that these actions were not merely the impulsive expression of Moses' wrath but rather constituted a standard symbolic procedure for declaring a covenant broken. The enforced drinking of the powder-strewn water represented the exposure of the guilty to the threatened curses of the covenant. Compare the jealousy ordeal of Numbers 5:23f., in which it is again a matter of a broken vow.

[41] See Sefireh I, face C, 17ff., and Sefireh II, face C, 1ff.

[42] A comparison has naturally been made with the pillar associated with Jacob's covenantal vow, which he said should be "God's house" (Gen. 28:18-22). Cf. J. A. Fitzmyer, "The Aramaic Inscriptions of Sefire I and II," *Journal of the American Oriental Society*, LXXXI, 3 (1961), 214. This covenant-bethel phenomenon also invites attention to the fundamental character of the altar in Israel as the dwelling place of Yahweh where he recorded his covenant name and beyond the Old Testament altar to the Christ, who in his incarnation was given for a covenant of the people (Isa. 42:6; 49:8) and was at once the temple and the Word of God. Cf., too, Exodus 24:4ff.; Deuteronomy 27:4-8; Joshua 8:30ff.; 24:25-27.

command you, neither shall ye diminish *ought* from it."[43]

These facts stand in diametrical opposition to the whole modern approach to the Book of Deuteronomy. According to current speculations Deuteronomy was produced by an extended process of modification and enlargement of a pliable tradition. The most relevant evidence, however, indicates that once treaty documents like Deuteronomy had been prepared for a special historical occasion, they would not be susceptible to ready modification. They were, in fact, protected from any alteration, erasure, or expansion by the most specific, solemn, and severe sanctions. The force of these facts is intensified for the Deuteronomic treaty by the reverence which the Israelites would have had for it not simply as a sealed and sanctioned covenant but as, in truth, the very word of God revealed to them from heaven.

Now that the form-critical data compel the recognition of the antiquity not merely of this or that element within Deuteronomy but of the Deuteronomic treaty in its integrity, any persistent insistence on a final edition of the book around the seventh century B.C. can be nothing more than a vestigial hypothesis, no longer performing a significant function in Old Testament criticism. Is it too much to hope that modern higher criticism's notorious traditionalism will no longer prove inertial enough to prevent the Deuteronomic bark from setting sail once more for its native port?

[43] Cf. Deuteronomy 12:32; Revelation 22:18, 19; and the familiar boast of Josephus in *Contra Apionem* 1:8.

Chapter Three

THE INTRUSION AND
THE DECALOGUE

The often canvassed subject of Old Testament ethics still beckons the investigator on in search of a more adequate solution of its peculiar complex of problems. In this search no other standard of righteousness is available to one who would think his Maker's thoughts after him than the standard which emerges in the description of the words and ways of God which have been inscripturated. But if it is in this very connection that the problems appear, what is the investigator to do? What, indeed, but to recognize that problematic as the biblical revelation of the divine activity might seem, it yet conveys a revelation of law. So will he give himself again to the exegesis of the Word in the conviction that the solution of the ethical problem must be one and the same as its accurate and adequate formulation. The attempt is, therefore, made here to seek a solution in terms of a somewhat fresh formulation of certain distinctive elements in the religion of the Old Testament.

The Concept of Intrusion

It is by tracing the unfolding eschatology of Scripture that we can most deftly unravel the strands of Old

Testament religion and discover what is essential and distinctive in it. For eschatology antedates redemption. The pattern for eschatology goes back to creation. Since the creature must pattern his ways after his Creator's, and since the Creator rested only after he had worked, it was a covenant of works which was proffered to Adam as the means by which to arrive at the consummation. In the sense that it was the door to the consummation, this original Covenant of Creation was eschatological.

That door, however, was never opened. It was not the Fall in itself that delayed the consummation. According to the conditions of the Covenant of Creation the prospective consummation was either/or. It was either eternal glory by covenantal confirmation of original righteousness or eternal perdition by covenant-breaking repudiation of it. The Fall, therefore, might have been followed at once by a consummation of the curse of the covenant. The delay was due rather to the principle and purpose of divine compassion by which a new way of arriving at the consummation was introduced, the way of redemptive covenant with common grace as its historical corollary.

For the present thesis it is especially significant that the delay and common grace are coterminous. In saying this we would not lose sight of the positive contribution of common grace to the new eschatological program. Common grace, whose mercies are real while they last, provides the field of operation for redemptive grace, and its material too. The delay associated with common grace makes possible a consummation involving an extensive revelation of the divine perfections, a glorified paradise as well as a lake of fire. This delay is not the delay of mere postponement but the delay of gestation. Nevertheless, it is at the same time true that consummation and commonness between elect and reprobate are mutually exclusive. In this limited sense common grace may be called the antithesis of the consummation, and as such it epitomizes this world-age as one during which the consummation is abeyant.

Because of the Fall the gestation-delay, the entire birth process that at last produces the consummation, is characterized by pain and sorrow. The whole creation groans and travails in pain together until now. But it is the consummation-child himself who particularly interests us. We suggest that he might well be named Perez. For he breaks through beforehand, making a breach for himself. That is, the Covenant of Redemption all along the line of its administration, more profoundly in the New Testament but already in the Old Testament, is a coming of the Spirit, an intrusion of the power, principles, and reality of the consummation into the period of delay. Breaking through first of all in the Old Testament period, the Intrusion finds itself in an age which is by the divine disposition of history, or, more specifically, by the divine administration of the Covenant of Redemption, an age of preparation for a later age of fulfillment and finality. Its appearing, therefore, is amid earthly forms which at once suggest, yet veil, the ultimate glory. Not to be obscured is the fact that within this temporary shell of the Intrusion there is a permanent core. The pattern of things earthly embodies realized eschatology, an actual projection of the heavenly reality. It is the consummation which, intruding into the time of delay, anticipates itself.

As for the peculiar forms of the Intrusion in the Old Testament age, they have a pattern coherent and comprehensive—for things must always be done decently and in order in the house of God. Taking for a moment an Old Testament standpoint and viewing these forms as belonging to the reality that *is* in Old Testament times, we may say that they also point to a reality that was (as an archetype in the heavens) and that is to come (in the Messianic age). They are antitype[1] in relation to the reality that was. They are sacramental symbol in relation

[1] *antitypa tōn alēthinōn* (Heb. 9:24).

to the core of the present Old Testament Intrusion of that reality. And they are type in relation to that reality as it is to come, when Messiah comes.

When the Old Testament forms are classified as type, their antitypes[2] are found in the present phase of the new covenant as well as in the eternal state, so epoch-making in the unfolding of the Intrusion is the revelation in the Son. However, the apocalypse of Jesus Christ and his kingdom is still in the category of Intrusion rather than perfect consummation, as is signalized by the fact that the present age is still characterized by common grace, the epitome of the delay. The identification of the new covenant with the consummation keeps pace with the stages in the exaltation of the Son of Man; and while we see him sitting on the right hand of power, we have not yet seen him coming in the clouds of heaven. Hence, there is not yet a corresponding antitype for every element of Old Testament typology. Certain Old Testament types find their antitype in the age introduced by the first coming of Christ, and, indeed, only there in some cases (e.g., the sacrifice of the Passover lamb). But the fulfillment of other Old Testament types is realized only in the world to come (e.g., the actual possession of the promised land by the people of God). While, therefore, the Old Testament is an earlier edition of the final reality than is the present age of the new covenant, and not so intensive, it is on its own level a more extensive edition, especially when considered in its own most fully developed form, viz., the Israelite theocracy.

[2] Some confusion arises in the terminology through the double use of the word "antitype" to signify both that the Old Testament is the copy of the prior heavenly pattern and that the New Testament reality corresponds to the earlier Old Testament pattern. Thus, not only are both Old Testament and New Testament antitype (although in different senses), but the Old Testament is both type and antitype (again from different points of view). Possibly it would be better, then, to style the Old Testament forms simply as "copies" when viewed in relation to the things in the heavens. Cf. Hebrews 9:23, *hypodeigmata tōn en tois ouranois.*

To summarize thus far: Perez makes the breach in the Old Testament; that is, the consummation intrudes itself there. This Intrusion has realized eschatology as its core, while its symbolic surface (the sacramental aspect thereof excepted) forms a typical picture of eschatology not yet realized. In the recognition of the true character of core and shell and in the further recognition that the core is always present within the shell lies the proper understanding of much in the Old Testament.

The Intrusion and Ethics

When we survey the Old Testament, a divinely sanctioned pattern of action emerges which is not consonant with the customary application of the law of God according to the principle of common grace. It will be our purpose to show that this ethical pattern is congenial to biblical religion by relating it to the Intrusion phenomenon which we have found to be an integral element in the Old Testament.

Biblical laws have been classified according to their ground as laws founded: (1) on the nature of God; (2) on permanent relations of men in their present state of existence; (3) on temporary relations of men or conditions of society; and (4) altogether on positive commands of God.[3] Discussing the question of how far the laws contained in the Bible may be dispensed with, Hodge says that the laws of group 1 are immutable; that the laws of group 2 may be set aside by the authority of God; and that the laws of groups 3 and 4 are mutable, the positive laws of the Old Testament being, as a matter of fact, now abolished together with those laws of group 3 which were designed exclusively for the Hebrews living under the theocracy.

[3] See C. Hodge, *Systematic Theology* (Grand Rapids, 1940), III, 267-269; cf. W. B. Green, "Ethics of the Old Testament," *Princeton Theological Review*, XXVII, 2 (1929), 179-181.

It is to be observed, however, that these categories are not mutually exclusive and that, therefore, there may be more complexity in the application of a given law than this simple formulation of the problem of mutability suggests. Two of these categories may be involved as multiple aspects of one law which may then have both a mutable and an immutable aspect. To illustrate, though laws five through ten in the Decalogue are grounded on permanent relations of men in their present state of existence, they are also founded on the nature of God. For they simply apply to specific cases the grand principle that man must reflect the moral glory of God on a finite scale. This principle is immutable because it concerns the relationship of man to God. On the other hand, the relations governed by this immutable principle are themselves mutable.

In the present age we may say that the essence of laws five through ten is that we are to love our neighbor as ourselves, and the answer to the question, "Who is my neighbor?", is the parable of the good Samaritan. But beyond this life that parable will no longer serve as the answer to that question. Then Lazarus must not so much as dip the tip of his finger in water to cool the tongue of him who is in anguish in the flame. The law of heaven requires that Lazarus pass him by on the other side. Not to take pleasure in his anguish (for Lazarus has been renewed in the image of God, not of Satan), but nonetheless to pass him by whom heaven's Lord must command, "Depart from me, thou cursed." The neighbor relationship envisaged in the parable of the good Samaritan has, therefore, a *terminus ad quem* at the limit of the present state of existence.

The unbeliever is the believer's neighbor today; but the reprobate is not the neighbor of the redeemed hereafter for the reason that God will set a great gulf between them. God, whose immutable nature it is to hate evil, withdrawing all favor from the reprobate, will himself hate them as sin's finished products. And if the redeemed in glory are to fulfill their duty of patterning their ways after God's, they will have to change their attitude toward the unbeliever from one of neighborly love to one of perfect hatred, which is a holy, not malicious passion. Just because the grand principle which underlies laws five through ten is immutable, the application of these laws must be changed in accordance with the changes in the intracreational relationships for which they legislate.

Now it appears that there was introduced in the Old Testament age a pattern of conduct akin to that found in prophetic portrayals of the kingdom of God beyond the present age of common grace. Our thesis is that this Old Testament ethical pattern is an aspect of the Intrusion. Included in it are both anticipations of God's judgment curse on the reprobate and of his saving grace in blessing his elect.

Possible misunderstandings may be forestalled by making certain observations at once. First, the demands of this Intrusion ethics in the Old Testament are not of a lower or laxer order. Quite the contrary, it was only in union with the highest outreach of faith that there could be true compliance with the demands of this ethics. Second, this concept of Intrusion ethics is not prejudicial to the permanent validity of the moral law of Moses. The distinction made is not one of different standards but of the application of a constant standard under significantly different conditions. It is evident that such a distinction must be made between the period of common grace in general and the age of the consummation. The only proposal beyond that made here is that there are anticipations of that distinction and, to that extent, an anticipatory abrogation of the principle of common grace during the Old Testament age. Finally, this concept of Intrusion ethics does not obscure the unity of the Covenant of Redemption throughout its various administrations. It does bring into bolder relief the basic structure of that covenant in its historical unfolding and in so doing inevitably displays its essential unity.

Intrusion of Judgment Curse

The Imprecations in the Psalms

In justification of the imprecations in the Psalms (see, e.g., Pss. 7, 35, 55, 59, 69, 79, 109 and 137) it is necessary to point out that the welfare of man is not the chief end of man; that we sinful creatures have no inherent rights which our holy Maker must respect; that accordingly, God may, without violating any obligation, take any man's life at any time and in any way; and that it is one with this for God to inspire the Psalmist to pray that he should do so in a particular instance, the prayer itself being altogether proper since it is divinely inspired. It is also helpful to indicate that the Psalmist expresses hatred of others and prays for their destruction not in a bitter spirit of personal vindictiveness but out of concern for the honor of God's name, which had been despised, and from love of God's kingdom, which had been opposed in that enmity displayed by the objects of the imprecations toward the Psalmist as one who represented that kingdom. However, when all this has been said by way of explanation and defense, the significance of the imprecations has not yet been fully appreciated.

Another important side of the picture can be brought into view by the observation that normally the believer's attitudes toward the unbeliever are conditioned by the principle of common grace. During the historical process of differentiation which common grace makes possible, before the secret election of God is unmistakably manifested at the great white throne, the servants of Christ are bound by his charge to pray for the good of those who despitefully use and persecute them. Our Lord rebuked the Boanerges when they contemplated consuming the Samaritans with fire from heaven (Luke 9:54; cf. Mark 3:17). We may not seek to destroy those for whom, perchance, Christ has died.

But in the final judgment the Lord will not rebuke

James and John if they make similar requests. Then it will be altogether becoming for the saint to desire God's wrath to descend upon his unbelieving enemy. No longer will there be the possibility that the enemy of the saint is the elect of God. Then the grain harvest will be ripe for the gathering of the Son of Man and the clusters of the vine will be fully ripe for the great winepress of the wrath of God.

We must distinguish an ethics of the consummation from an ethics of common grace, and the imprecations in the Psalms confront us unexpectedly with a pattern of conduct which conforms to the ethics of the consummation. Since it is intruded by inspiration it constitutes a divine abrogation, within a limited sphere, of the ethical requirements normally in force during the course of common grace. What is required is that we cease stumbling over this as though it were a problem and recognize it as a feature of the divine administration of the Covenant of Redemption in the Old Testament, a feature that displays the sovereign authority of the covenant God. It is also bright with promise for the future of his kingdom and people; for, to make explicit the obvious, this ethical intrusion appropriately attaches itself to the activity of persons and institutions which were types of things to come in the age of the consummation. The ethical principles themselves belong to the core of consummation reality within the shell of things typical.

The Conquest of Canaan

Another familiar Old Testament ethical problem is that of justifying the Israelite dispossession and extermination of the Canaanites over against the sixth and eighth words of the Decalogue. Defense might be attempted by comparing the function of the ordinary state when, acting through its officers against criminals or through its military forces against offending nations, it destroys life and exacts reparations. The proper performance of this function is not a violation but a fulfillment of the provisions of common grace. For in God's dealing with mankind in common grace he has authorized the state as "an avenger for wrath to him that doeth evil."

Now it is true that Israel's army was also an avenger for wrath. But while an analogy may be recognized between the two things being compared, the conclusion cannot be avoided that radically different principles are at work. For if Israel's conquest of Canaan were to be adjudicated before an assembly of nations acting according to the provisions of common grace, that conquest would have to be condemned as an unprovoked aggression and, moreover, an aggression carried out in barbarous violation of the requirement to show all possible mercy even in the proper execution of justice. It would not avail the counsel for the defense to claim that by a divine promise originally made to Abraham and afterwards reiterated to his descendants the land was rightfully Israel's, nor to insist that the iniquity of the Amorites was full and cried to heaven for judgment, nor to advise the court that the conquest was undertaken and waged according to specific directions of Israel's God to Moses and Joshua. Such facts would have no legal significance for the international tribunal judging solely by the principle of common grace.

It will only be with the frank acknowledgment that ordinary ethical requirements were suspended and the ethical principles of the last judgment intruded that the divine promises and commands to Israel concerning Canaan and the Canaanites come into their own. Only so can the conquest be justified and seen as it was in truth—not murder, but the hosts of the Almighty visiting upon the rebels against his righteous throne their just deserts—not robbery, but the meek inheriting the earth.

It was earlier maintained that Intrusion ethics required of him who would obey its demands the highest outreach of faith. Thus, in the case of the conquest, showing mercy to Canaanite women and children would not have been rising above a condescending, permissive decree to the heights of compliance with a loftier standard. It would have been falling, through lack of faith, into the abyss of disobedience. As a matter of fact, was it not the great men of faith, a Moses, a Joshua, a Caleb, who prosecuted the conquest with vigor? And was it not in consequence of spiritual declension in Israel that they soon began to spare and make peace with those Canaanites who were left in the land to try them? The conquest, with the pattern of Old Testament action it exemplifies, was not, as it is so often stigmatized, an instance in the ethical sphere of arrested evolution but rather of anticipated eschatology.

Other Intrusions of Judgment

Ethical anticipations of the judgment of the reprobate are found in cases involving all the rest of commandments five through ten, excepting the seventh for the reason that "every sin that a man doeth is without the body; but he that committeth fornication sinneth against his own body" (1 Cor. 6:18).

According to the fifth commandment, Rahab owed obedience to the civil authorities of Jericho. When information was requested of her concerning the enemy spies, it was, according to ordinary ethics, her duty to supply it. Nevertheless, by faith she united herself to the cause of the theocracy and so played her part as an agent of the judgment-conquest which was typical of the final judgment, denying to the obstinate foes of God that respect for their authority which was their due under common grace. For so doing, Rahab receives inspired approbation (Heb. 11:31; Jas. 2:25).

By the same token, the enemies of the theocracy lost the ordinary right to hear the truth as that is guaranteed by the ninth commandment. Insofar, therefore, as the theocratic agent did not deny God (or, to put it differently, did not violate the immutable principles of the first three laws of the Decalogue), he might with perfect ethical propriety deceive such as had hostile intent against the theocracy. Accordingly, there is no necessity from the analogy of Scripture to avoid what seems the plain impression of certain passages to the effect that such deception was practiced with divine approval (e.g., the deception of Pharaoh by the Hebrew midwives; Exod. 1:15-21) or even by divine command (e.g., Samuel's deception of Saul; 1 Sam. 16:2).

In the abstract it is possible to distinguish between losing the right to hear the truth and the speaking of an untruth, and then to hold that the theocratic agent might not deceive even though the enemy of the theocracy had forfeited his right to be informed of the truth. But in the actual historical struggle, the two might, at times at least, become inseparable. Saul, for example, had no right to be told that David was being anointed to replace him. Now if we abstract Samuel's conduct that day in Bethlehem from its historical setting, we might explain his silence concerning his primary purpose as simply a withholding of information. But that would, indeed, be an abstraction and not the reality. Samuel's action was in the living context of Saul's actively hostile interest in it. His strategy was framed with the specific intent of parrying the thrust of that enmity. To do that successfully, mere silence would not suffice, for his action cried out for an explanation and Saul was bound to have one. Only the positive step of creating a false impression could achieve Samuel's purpose, and he took that step by making prominent the sacrifice. Certainly, in the text itself, the command to take along a heifer and to supervise a sacrifice is given as the immediate response to Samuel's desire to avert Saul's suspicion. That Samuel actually planned to sacrifice once he had been so directed is irrelevant. The point to be observed is the immediate purpose of the Lord in commanding him to sacrifice in the first place.

It was noticed above that an analogy exists between the state's judicial use of the sword and Israel's conquest of Canaan, even though the latter cannot be justified in terms of the principle of common grace. So in the present instance an analogy obtains between the deception employed by a theocratic representative against an active opponent of the theocracy and the deception rightly practiced by the ordinary state, through the agency of a military officer in a skillful tactic in a just war, for example.

In cases of Intrusion ethics which involve the eighth word of the Decalogue, the tenth word may also be involved. The discussion of the imprecations in the Psalms has already indicated that even the inward feelings of the theocratic agents could by inspiration be brought within the sphere of the Intrusion. Must we not, then, also regard the Hebrew man of faith engaged in the conquest as coveting the land of the Canaanites, at least to the degree that he was obeying God's battle charge from his heart and with understanding? Though that would ordinarily be to sin against one who was his neighbor, this was one of the instances where the neighbor concept operative under common grace was abrogated by divine ordering in favor of the neighbor concept of the final judgment and beyond, according to which God's enemies are not the elect's neighbors. When the Old Testament believer, at the Lord's command, took his typical stand beyond common grace, to covet the property of the unbeliever was to be in harmony with God's purpose to perfect his kingdom.

In the area of penal sanctions against offending covenant members, the Intrusion principle again manifests itself. It is especially significant that among the offenses for which the death penalty was prescribed are violations of the first four laws of the Decalogue (see, e.g., Exod. 31:14f.; 35:2 [cf. Num. 15:32ff.]; Lev. 24:16; Deut. 13:5ff.; 17:2ff.). In the present age such violations are subject to ecclesiastical discipline, but the sword may not be wielded by either church or state in punishment of such offenders, according to the principle of common grace. In the consummation, however, the portion of those who do not obey these laws from the heart will be "the second death." It is then consummation justice that was intruded when death was prescribed for religious offenses in Israel, the kingdom where the consummation was typically anticipated. The Intrusion appears most vividly in those instances where the infliction of death was not the act of a theocratic official but of God (see, e.g., Num. 11:1f.; 16:31ff.; 2 Kings 2:24).

Intrusion of Redemptive Blessing

The Theocracy and the Nations

Apropos of the fifth word, it is in this New Testament age not a legitimate function of a civil government to endorse and support religious establishments. This principle applies equally to the Christian church; for though its invisible government is theocratic with Christ sitting on David's throne in the heavens and ruling over it, yet its visible organization, in particular as it is related to civil powers, is so designed that it takes a place of only common privilege along with other religious institutions within the framework of common grace. It is quite otherwise in the consummation. Then every dominion and power in heaven, on earth, and under the earth, must do obeisance to the Christ of God. Moreover, it is this ultimate state of affairs that is found intruded into the Old Testament dispensation in connection with the Israelite theocracy, which typified the perfected kingdom of God.

While this typical kingdom of heaven was in existence, the other nations on earth stood in a peculiar relation to it. We are informed, for example, that "the Lord stirred up the spirit of Cyrus, king of Persia, so that he made a proclamation throughout his kingdom" in which he professed to have received a charge from the Lord God of heaven to build him a house in Jerusalem (Ezra 1:1ff.).

Later Persian monarchs also gave positive support to the building and maintaining of the temple of the restoration and, moreover, contributed from government funds for its ritual. The famous Cyrus cylinder reveals that Cyrus' policy toward the religion of Israel was in keeping with a general policy of restoring exiled nations and their religious cults, but that does not affect the point that it was by divine instigation that Cyrus actively supported the organized religion of Israel.[4] This procedure is obviously not normative for civil governments in the New Testament dispensation. What we have here is a case of Intrusion ethics in connection with the Israelite theocracy as a type of the heavenly kingdom into which "the kings of earth do bring their glory and honor" (Rev. 21:24).

The "Sacrifice" of Isaac

The divine command to Abraham to slay Isaac confronted him with a contradiction of previous revelation concerning human life, revelation later formulated in the sixth word of the Decalogue. It is the Creator's prerogative to assign such significance to his creatures as he will, and it is man's duty to accept the divine interpretation. The more unaccountable to man the divine interpretation might be, the better calculated it is to bring to the fore in man's consciousness the necessity of thinking and living covenantally, that is, in the obedience of personal devotion to his God. As God had given a special meaning to one of the trees of the garden, making it, exceptionally, a tree of forbidden fruit, and as God gave a peculiar significance to certain meats in the ceremonial of the Old Testament, making them unclean, so now God was redefining the life of Isaac, declaring it the life to be sacrificed.

---

[4] That Cyrus' policy toward Israel is to be regarded as proper would seem evident from the biblical assessment of his historical role (cf. esp. Isa. 44:28; 45:1-5).

Faced with this new word of God, Abraham must not make an abstract idol out of the customary prohibition against human sacrifice but must listen to his Father's voice.[5] If, in deference to the idol dictum, Abraham rejects God's interpretation of Isaac's life at this juncture, he will find consistency demanding of him when he hears the word of the gospel that he reject the interpretation God gives there of the life of his Son. The word of the Cross will be a stumbling block to him.

It was the ethics of the Cross, itself an intrusion of final judgment into mid-history, that was intruded into the Old Testament age in the divine command to sacrifice Isaac. The provision of the sacrificial substitute once Abraham had manifested the obedience of faith advises us of the inadequacy of sinful human life for making atonement. God had not defined Isaac's life as the life that was actually to be sacrificed as an atonement for sin. Meanwhile, Abraham's confrontation with the Intrusion's demand had served to try the father of believers whether he was prepared to live by every word that proceeded out of the mouth of God.

The Marriage of Hosea

The interpretation of the marriage of the prophet Hosea (Hos. 1 and 3) has been perplexed by the ethical

---

[5] Since the Father speaks to his children today only in the words of the completed Scriptures, we are never tested in the peculiar manner of Abraham's trial of faith; that is, there are now no immediate divine revelations whose authority we might defy by idolizing previous revelation. It is also true, however, that the "now," the present dispensation, is not a closed and perpetual order but is an age open to the final divine in-breaking and will be terminated by the coming of the day of the Lord. The child of the covenant, therefore, must live in expectant hope of "the appearing of the glory of the great God and our Saviour Jesus Christ" and must, when confronted with that ultimate theophany, be ready to heed the new demands of his God even though they annul Scriptural requirements in force during the age just a moment ago waxed old and vanished away.

problem with which certain views are believed to be entangled. While accepting the view that only one woman is intended throughout, and she a harlot before the marriage, it is not our purpose here to defend this view in detail, whether in its realistic, visionary, or symbolical variety, but only to point out that there is no insoluble ethical problem preventing its adoption.

According to the Mosaic law, prostitution was one of the violations of the seventh commandment that required exclusion from the theocratic congregation (Lev. 19:29; Deut. 23:17). It was certainly implied in this that a harlot might not be espoused by a covenant member. Nevertheless, in contradiction of this ordinary requirement, the Lord commanded Hosea to marry the harlot, Gomer. In so doing, God was again anticipating an ethical principle entailed in his saving of the elect.

Like Abraham, Hosea must not abstract one legal word from the eschatological context of divine revelation and make it an idol absolute that forbids him to obey his Father when he speaks anew in the startling terms of Intrusion ethics. If Hosea is offended by the command to take Gomer to wife now, he will be unable later to participate in the great marriage celebration of the Lamb. But blessed is Hosea if he is not offended, for then he will anticipatively exhibit in his marriage the consummation of God's grace to be realized when the holy One and undefiled receives a church-bride composed of a multitude of defiled sinners to be his own.

Conclusion

Enough has, perhaps, been presented now to display how, in union with the phenomenon of typology, there was during the Old Testament dispensation an anticipatory exercise of the ethics of the world to come. Ignorance of this is fraught with danger for the formulator of Christian ethics, for he will be likely to found matters of present Christian duty upon cases of Intrusion ethics. And thereby he would become unwittingly guilty of assuming the prerogative of God to abrogate the principle of common grace.

One further similar caution in closing: the recognition that the hour comes when it will be our duty to hate the unbeliever must not diminish and ought to intensify our efforts to show him the love of Christ in the hour that now is. When our Father shall say, "It is done," we must listen to his voice. But if we are listening to him today, we are still seeking by his grace to be good Samaritans.

Chapter Four

THE OLD TESTAMENT ORIGINS OF THE GOSPEL GENRE

Was the gospel genre a creation of the New Testament evangelists or can it be traced back beyond the first century A.D.? In dealing with this form-critical problem we soon find that we are involved with more than the literary form of the gospels. Our form-critical investigation confronts us with fundamental questions about their essential nature, purpose, and message. And to be involved with such questions about the gospels is to be engaged in an analysis of the basic character and structure of biblical religion.

A certain amount of ambiguity attends the use of the term "genre" in form-critical studies.[1] Varying combinations of things like structural pattern, setting, content, mood, and intention are regarded by different form critics as constitutive of genre. The problem of definition may be somewhat simplified at least if we restrict the term to whole documents. The constitutive components of genre as the term will be used here with reference to the gospels are overall form and societal-religious function.

[1] Cf. R. Knierim, "Old Testament Form Criticism Reconsidered," *Interpretation*, XXVII, 4 (1973), 435-468.

172

To date no scholarly consensus, at least no positive consensus, has emerged from the extensive efforts to identify the canonical gospels with some genre attested in earlier literary tradition. After a perceptive survey of studies along this line, R. H. Gundry endorses the conclusion that from a first-century standpoint the gospels must be pronounced a literary novelty. In his judgment, therefore, it is not legitimate to speak of a gospel genre except in the sense that the four New Testament gospels themselves originated such a genre.[2]

At the heart of the problem is the fact that the gospels consist of two very different kinds of material: teaching discourse and historical narrative. They contain accounts of both the words and works of Jesus. Considerable difficulty is already encountered in the attempt to classify each of these two types of material individually in terms of earlier literary forms, quite apart from the problem of accounting for them in combination. The discourses of Jesus include sapiential, legal, polemical, apocalyptic, and other kinds of pronouncements. No single form-critical classification that has been suggested, such as sayings of the wise or manual of community order, manages to comprehend all of this variety. Neither has the search for a specific form of narrative with which to identify the gospel records of the works of Jesus met with success. In particular, the attempt to relate these gospel narratives to aretalogical biography has proven a disappointment on both literary and theological grounds. But the real problem still comes when we try to account for the total form of the gospels, including what they report of both the deeds and sayings of Jesus. In the opinion of the form critics generally, literary antecedents

[2] Robert H. Gundry, "Recent Investigations into the Literary Genre 'Gospel,'" *New Dimensions in New Testament Study* (ed. R. N. Longenecker and M. C. Tenney; Grand Rapids, 1974), pp. 97-114. Cf. Ralph P. Martin, *New Testament Foundations*, Volume 1 (Grand Rapids, 1975), pp. 16ff.

are apparently not to be found for the gospel form taken as a whole.

Having reached a negative conclusion as to the existence of literary antecedents of the complete form of the gospels, the form critics have turned to the historical circumstances out of which these documents arose for the explanation of their diverse contents and the evidently new literary form they represent. Some have seen the different kinds of material contained in the gospels as reflecting the variety of activity and concern that made up the life and mission of the early Christian communities to which the gospels were directed. Unfortunately, the tendency of form-critical studies along these lines has been to attribute to the church a creative role with regard to the substance of the gospel tradition.

The more conservative form critics have also appreciated the importance of the ecclesiastical *sitz im leben* of the gospels. They have recognized that understanding of the church audience to which a gospel was addressed can help to account for its particular Christological interests and its distinctive selection and arrangement of the available data. The emphasis of the conservatives, however, has fallen on the gospels not as church documents but as lives of Jesus, and they have tended to explain the gospels' peculiar configuration of narratives and discourses, the macrostructure common to all of them, as due ultimately to the actual nature of Jesus' historical career. Jesus and his mission confronted the world with a unique complex of historical phenomena and it was this uniqueness of Jesus and his redemptive accomplishment that led to the unique Christian kerygma and thus to a new literary genre as that kerygma found documentary expression in the gospels of Matthew, Mark, Luke, and John.

The Book of Exodus and the Gospel Genre

We may readily agree that it would have been fitting for the revelation of the Messiah's mission to be given in the form of a brand new literary genre. But is it after all really the case that the gospel genre was a creation of the first century A.D.?

The Qumran documents have provided fresh evidence of the familiar fact that the Judaism that formed the immediate background of the New Testament appropriated all kinds of literary forms from the Old Testament—apocalypse, history, testament, psalm, and a variety of didactic and legal genres. The suggestion that the New Testament evangelists adopted a genre prominent in their Old Testament Scriptures would, therefore, be altogether compatible with general literary practice in the historical context in which the gospels originated.

In the search for the origins of the gospel genre, the form critics have indeed traced the trajectories of various kinds of gospel materials to Old Testament sources. Nevertheless, they have overlooked the obvious, if I see it aright, in failing to find the origins of the gospel genre as such in the Old Testament, specifically, in the second volume of the Pentateuch.[3] For the Book of Exodus appears to have the same thematic focus and to exhibit comprehensively the same literary structure as the gospels. What I hope to show then is, in a word, that the Book of Exodus is an Old Testament gospel—the Gospel of Moses.[4]

Coming to the question of the gospel genre from a background of more specialized concern with the form-critical questions of the Old Testament, particularly of the Pentateuch, what has impressed me is the similarity of the key problem in the two cases. In both the Penta-

[3] The section of the Pentateuch we call the Book of Exodus is marked off as a unit in itself by the distinctive contents and form of the two sections that immediately bound it (Genesis and Leviticus). Even according to modern higher critical views of the origin of Exodus, it had, of course, emerged and been regarded as a discrete literary entity long before the production of the New Testament gospels.

[4] The present chapter carries a step further a suggestion I made in *The Westminster Theological Journal*, XXXII, 2 (1970), 198 (cf. above, pp. 71ff.).

teuch (or more narrowly, Exodus) and the gospels the problem is one of explaining the combination of two major kinds of literary material. Moreover, the two kinds of material are very much the same in the two cases—historical narrative and legislation in the Pentateuch, historical narrative and authoritative sayings in the gospels. The very problem that most perplexes the New Testament form critic at this point thus turns out to be a clue directing him to the goal of his quest.

In the course of the literary criticism of the Pentateuch the documentary theorists, as is well known, have seized upon the difference between narrative and legislative materials as a criterion for the identification of the hypothetical Pentateuchal sources. The partitioning of the Book of Exodus between the putative priestly source and the supposed narrative sources has followed for the most part the lines of distinction between legal ordinance and historical narrative. But form-critical study has now disclosed the actual generic unity and identity of the documentary combination of history and law.[5] This combination was a regular feature of the second millennium B.C. treaty genre. After a preamble introducing the suzerain-author of the treaty, an historical prologue reviewed the past relationships of the covenant partners and this was followed by a law section defining the vassal's duties. The Mosaic covenants, the Decalogue and Deuteronomy, appropriated this international treaty form and thus the history-law complex is found in them too. The combination of narrative and legislation in the Book of Exodus does not, therefore, betray a multiplicity of sources behind that document. The conclusion warranted by the form-critical facts is rather that the treaty form adopted by Moses in the Decalogue and Deuteronomy exercised a pervasive influence as he shaped the larger Pentateuchal composition in which he set those treaty texts. It is because Exodus, though not a treaty as such, is an adap-

[5] Cf. above, p. 53.

tive development of the treaty, a creative by-form of the treaty form, that it contains history and law in the peculiar combination that it does.

As observed above, the distinctive combination of narrative and authoritative words is a feature of Exodus and the New Testament gospels alike. As soon as our attention is drawn, whether by this observation or along some other route, to the literary similarity of the gospels to Exodus with its covenantal orientation, the principal elements of that parallelism quickly make themselves apparent and we find that the pieces of the gospel genre picture begin to fall into place. What then are these structural features that Exodus and the gospels have in common and justify our speaking of them as a single genre?

In the structure of the gospels the most prominent feature is the long section devoted to the passion narratives. Starting with the transfiguration event (in the Synoptics) and continuing through the resurrection-ascension records, it extends about half the total length of each of the gospels.[6] All that precedes in the gospel story clearly has its face set steadfastly towards this climax in Jerusalem. The passion narratives thus dominate the gospel form thematically and quantitatively.

This feature has its counterpart in the Book of Exodus in the dominant position occupied there by the account of the inauguration of the Sinaitic Covenant. Beginning at Exodus 19, this climactic section continues on through the entire last half of the book to its conclusion. Here is the record of the awesome scene of theophany and covenant ratification, the divine revelation of the provisions of the covenant, the erection of the tabernacle-residence of the heavenly Suzerain, and the enthronement of his

---

[6]This applies to the Gospel of John as well as to the Synoptics, although John omits the transfiguration episode. On the latter as the opening of the passion narratives, cf. N. B. Stonehouse, *The Witness of Matthew and Mark to Christ* (Philadelphia, 1944), p. 157.

glory there in the midst of the covenant community. All the events narrated in the first part of the book lead upwards to this covenantal engagement of Israel at the mountain of God as their high goal. The very topography of the Israelites' journey brings into high relief the ascending literary movement of the book as they proceed from the river valley of Egypt through the depths of the sea, thence along the rising terrain to the heights of Sinai, the lofty setting of the covenant consummation of Exodus 19-40.

The correspondence between the dominant second halves of Exodus and the gospels is a matter of content as well as form. For the underlying theme of the passion narratives in the gospels is precisely that of their Exodus counterpart—the inauguration of the covenant. As we shall want to observe further below, the basically covenantal orientation of the sufferings, death, and resurrection of Christ as presented in these narratives is evidenced by explicitly covenantal terminology and, less directly but nonetheless most effectively, by the gospels' extensive appropriation of the exodus-Sinai experiences of Israel as a typological model in the delineation of the Messianic history. Incidentally, geographical peaks mark the literary heights in the gospels too. The climactic passion narratives are bracketed by the mounts of transfiguration and ascension, the former of these mountaintop episodes being most realistically related to the parallel Sinai-event of the Book of Exodus by the very presence of Moses.

There is a second obvious and major structural correspondence between the gospels and Exodus. It is one that involves the entire first halves of these compositions leading up to the climactic episodes of covenant ratification. In these opening sections both Exodus and the gospels recount the life or at least the public career of the covenant mediator. These accounts of the missions of Moses and Jesus are, of course, not confined to the first halves of the documents but continue on through the covenant ratification events related in the second halves. Indeed, it is supremely in the ratification episodes that the mediatorial office is fulfilled. Actually then this aspect of the structural parallelism comprehends Exodus and the gospels in their entireties.

The all-inclusive role of Moses as he is presented in the Book of Exodus is plainly that of mediator of the covenant. In the gospels, however, it is not so immediately apparent that the role of covenant mediator is the central and unifying category in the multi-faceted ministry of Jesus. But once it is recognized that the inauguration of the covenant is the governing motif of the passion narratives on which the gospels place such overwhelming emphasis and that covenant ratification is, therefore, to be seen as the culminating achievement towards which Jesus' earlier career moves, the centrality of the mediatorial office in the perspective of the gospels' total portrayal of Jesus and his work can be readily perceived.[7]

It is Jesus' office of covenant mediator that provides the natural and proper explanation of the combination of gospel discourse and gospel narrative that has proved so obstinate an obstacle in the gospel genre quest. For the covenant mediator is prophet as well as ruler and priest; he conveys the words of the Lord's covenant to his people, as well as rescuing them from their enemies and officiating at the ratification rites. The authoritative sayings of Jesus that are interspersed through the narratives of his saving acts are then clearly to be identified as the new covenant equivalents of the covenantal directives of Moses to Israel in Exodus and elsewhere in the Pentateuch.

The structural correspondences that have been noted between the gospels and Exodus are not peripheral but

---

[7] Even if one did not agree that covenant mediatorship is the controlling motif in the gospels' picture of Jesus' mission, he would still have to recognize that Exodus and the gospels are alike in that their overall outlines are unified by the story of a central protagonist, a great deliverer of God's people.

fundamental. They take into account the most conspicuous formal features of these documents, features that encompass their entire contents. Moreover, these formal features include distinctive material specifications. The parallelism between these compositions extends beyond the general features that have been mentioned; this is especially true of the material correspondence as to covenantal situation. But the foregoing general comparison of structure and content is an adequate enough basis for stating the conclusion that the New Testament gospels and the Book of Exodus are to be viewed as a single genre.

Obviously, every individual specimen of a given genre differs in various ways from all the others; each is to some extent an adaptive variation of the generic form. The flexibility of the gospel genre is displayed by the differences among the four New Testament gospels. As redaction criticism has emphasized, each evangelist had a distinctive Christological perspective which resulted in a distinctive total treatment of those narrative and discourse materials he had at his disposal. Two of the gospels contain accounts of the genealogy and birth of the covenant mediator, while the other two begin in other ways. Luke even made his gospel part one of a two-part work and gave the whole a dedicatory setting according to common formal conventions of his day. Such variations simply reflect the particular circumstances of the origin of each gospel and the special ecclesiastical situation to which each was addressed, as the kerygmatic approach has stressed. They do not forestall the identification of these four gospels as one genre.[8]

Although the differences between the Old Testament Book of Exodus and the New Testament gospels with respect to provenience and literary distinctives are certainly much more pronounced than the differences that

8Cf. Gundry, *op. cit.*, p. 114.

distinguish the New Testament gospels from one another, they are nevertheless not of such significance as to disallow the classification of Exodus with the others as a single genre. Definitions of literary genres cannot avoid a certain amount of arbitrariness at the edges of the idea. As I see it, the somewhat more flexible concept of genre one operates with if he identifies Exodus and the New Testament gospels as a single genre is hermeneutically more illuminating than the more rigid concept he adopts if he identifies them as different genres.

To suggest a provisional working definition: A document of the gospel genre is one that has as its literary center of gravity an account of the inauguration of a divine covenant, set within a record of the covenant mediator's career and of the law of the community promulgated by the mediator.

There is a functional component that should be added to our concept of the gospel genre. It is implicit in the formal-material elements already mentioned. We shall return to that but wish to take up at this point another feature in the gospels of special relevance for our thesis.

Moses-Exodus Typology in the Gospels

By the citation of Old Testament promise and prediction in their narration of Jesus' life, the New Testament evangelists show that they understand our Lord's mission to be the fulfillment of the Old Testament hope. They also make the connection with the Old Testament revelation by constructing their account of God's epochally new intervention through his Son in such a way as to bring out its typological relationship to the history of the old covenant. They present the saving acts of Christ as a new exodus led by a new Moses.[9]

Many special studies have dealt with various facets of

[9]Messianic prophecy in the Old Testament had already done this. The Qumran sect too regarded its experience as a new exodus.

this typological use of the Mosaic history in the gospels. Our survey of the matter here will be merely an outline sketch singling out a suggestive selection from among the possible instances of this rather pervasive feature of the gospels.

Our treatment of this vast area can afford to be somewhat tentative in detail since our primary thesis concerning the generic oneness of the gospels and the Book of Exodus rests squarely on the major structural parallels between them to which attention has already been called; it is not dependent on the evidence of exodus typology in the gospels. In fact, genre identification is not a matter of historical typology but of literary typicality. For example, the Book of Revelation contains a good deal of typological symbolism drawn from the history of the exodus, but it does not exhibit the broad formal-material literary parallelism to the Book of Exodus that we have found in the case of the gospels and, therefore, there is no question of identifying Revelation and Exodus as one genre. At the same time, although the gospels' use of the exodus model bears only indirectly on our thesis, it does offer support for our conclusion by confirming the fact that Jesus and his work are contemplated in the gospels from a perspective that is primarily and pervasively covenantal.

The numerous studies of the new Moses and new exodus imagery in the gospels that have been produced over the years have had scarcely any noticeable effect on the concurrent investigation of the gospel genre problem. This is so even though an occasional statement may be found in the typological studies to the effect that the Book of Exodus influenced the form as well as the content of the gospel story, or even that it influenced the broad structure of a particular New Testament gospel.[10]

10 Cf. Otto A. Piper, "Unchanging Promises," *Interpretation*, XI (1957), 16ff. and Jacob J. Enz, "The Book of Exodus as a Literary Type for the Gospel of John," *Journal of Biblical Literature*, LXXVI (1957), 208ff.

Perhaps the reason that those engaged in the gospel genre studies have not followed up on this clue is that the typological studies have not faced squarely the form-critical issues of genre definition or have even confused historical typology with literary typicality.

*   *   *   *   *

We will deal first with certain general themes found in the gospels' exposition of the Messianic salvation.

The word *exodos* (usually translated "departure") appears in the transfiguration episode at the very beginning of the Lucan passion narratives (Lk. 9:31). This "exodus" discussed by Moses and Elijah as they spoke with Jesus was soon to transpire at Jerusalem. Suggestions vary as to the precise stage in the Mosaic exodus and the parallel exodus of Jesus that is referred to by the term *exodos*: (a) The Israelites' departure from Egypt; and Jesus' departure from Jerusalem (cf. Rev. 11:8), the city doomed to desolation, on his way to Calvary (Matt. 27:32; Mk. 15:20; Lk. 23:26; Jn. 19:17), there to suffer outside the gate, in the wilderness (cf. Heb. 13:12). (b) The passage of the departing Israelites through the waters of the sea; and Jesus' undergoing of the baptismal ordeal of his passion (Matt. 20:22; Mk. 10:38; Lk. 12:50; cf. 1 Cor. 10:2). (c) The triumphant emergence of the Israelites from the sea, leaving behind the draconic enemy, pharaonic Egypt, buried in the sea; and Jesus' resurrection from the grave in victory over death and the Devil (cf. Heb. 13:20; Isa. 63:11ff.), with his subsequent leading of the disciples forth from Jerusalem (Lk. 24:50) to the mount of ascension. Perhaps the *exodos* of Luke 9:31 refers broadly to the whole death-resurrection complex. In that case, this striking term (the name of the Book of Exodus in the Septuagint) stands in the transfiguration account as a virtual heading for the entire passion narratives section introduced by that episode.

The Messianic exodus like its Mosaic type occurred in a

Passover context. The last supper constituted a bond between the Passover and the Cross, for it had the Passover feast for its matrix, while it sacramentally celebrated the sacrifice of Christ.[11] The association of the death of Jesus with the Passover is brought out most emphatically in the Gospel of John according to the view (which I find unacceptable) that John describes the crucifixion as taking place on the very day of the Passover sacrifice and that he does this with the intention not of providing chronology but of identifying Jesus' death typologically as the true Passover sacrifice. But the Cross of Jesus, like the Mosaic crossing of the sea, was in any case closely conjoined in time with the celebration of the Passover. A possible allusion to the Passover as an image of Jesus' sacrificial death is found in John the Forerunner's description of Jesus as "the lamb of God" (Jn. 1:29, 36), but the referent is not altogether certain.

The terminology of redemption emerges in the narrative of Moses' mission in the Book of Exodus (Exod. 6:6; 15:13).[12] It is the nature of the exodus as a deliverance from slavery that is in the foreground when it is characterized as a redemption. God heard the cry of the Israelites by reason of their foreign taskmasters; he remembered his covenant with the patriarchs (Exod. 2:24; 3:6-10); and he redeemed his people—he acquired them for himself again. Luke draws upon this exodus-redemption imagery in his gospel. He uses the language of redemption in his accounts of Jesus' nativity and youth (Lk. 1:68; 2:38). Thus, right from the beginning of his gospel, Luke puts the career of the Lord in an exodus setting. He indicates that Zacharias, father of John the Forerunner, echoing the words of God at the call of

[11] It is noteworthy from the viewpoint of literary analysis that the fact that a memorial feast was instituted on the eve of each exodus resulted in a narrative-disrupting insertion of legislation at a momentous juncture in the conflict (cf. Exod. 12:1ff.).

[12] Cf. Deuteronomy 7:8; 9:26; 13:5; 21:8. Genesis 48:16 is the only pre-exodus instance.

Moses (Exod. 3:6-8; cf. 2:24), prophetically interpreted the salvation to be accomplished by Jesus as a second exodus deliverance from the land of oppression in fulfillment of God's covenant with the patriarchs (Lk. 1:68-74; cf. Exod. 3:8; 5:23; 12:27; 18:4, 8ff.). Elsewhere in Luke's gospel the hope of the remnant in Israel, which was fastening itself upon Jesus for its realization, is summed up in the word "redemption" (Lk. 2:38; 24:21). Also, a saying of Jesus is recorded in which he calls the final eschatological deliverance a redemption (Lk. 21:28). It is in the Gospel of Luke too that the Nazareth synagogue episode is related, in which Jesus portrays his mission as the fulfillment of the Jubilee symbol (as channelled through the Messianic prophecy of Isa. 61:1ff.), the symbol of the ultimate redemption from slavery (Lk. 4:18ff.).

It was noted above that since the Lord's Supper was instituted during the Passover meal and as an adaptation of it for the church, the death of Jesus memorialized by the Supper is related to the Passover and, through the Passover, to the exodus as its context of meaning. The words of institution of the Supper also interpret the sacrifice of the Cross explicitly as a covenantal transaction (Matt. 26:28; Mk. 14:24; Lk. 22:20), and covenant is another exodus-related motif.[13] Covenant and exodus are inseparable in the Mosaic history. Indeed, according to the narrative in the Book of Exodus the establishment of the covenant at Sinai was the purpose and goal of the exodus process: Moses was to bring Israel out of Egypt so that they might proceed to the mount of God, there to enter as covenant vassals into the kingdom service of their

[13] This explicitly covenantal exposition of Jesus' death is in itself obviously the most direct evidence for the presence of the covenantal perspective in the passion narratives. But it is being cited at this point for the contribution it makes to the case we are developing in the present section of this essay for the extensive use of exodus typology in the gospels as an indirect argument for the primacy of the covenantal perspective of the gospels.

covenant Lord (Exod. 3:12; 4:23; and repeatedly; cf. Exod. 19:1).

More particularly, at the institution of the Lord's Supper Jesus called the blood of his imminent sacrificial death the "blood of the new covenant," so interpreting it in terms of the covenant-ratifying blood in the ritual described in Exodus 24:3-8 (cf. Heb. 9:20).[14] Since the symbol adopted by Jesus as the sign of his covenant blood was the sacramental cup of the transformed Passover meal, Jesus' death answers both to the sacrifice offered in preparation for the Passover and to the ratification sacrifices of the Sinaitic Covenant. Thus, the significance of the blood ceremonies that introduced and consummated the exodus-event fuse in the meaning of the Cross.

The covenant sacrifice at Sinai was followed by the covenant communion meal of Israel's elders in the presence of God on the mountain (Exod. 24:9-11). This aspect of the covenant-making at the Mosaic exodus is clearly present in the communion of the disciples with Jesus at the last supper, and again when the chosen witnesses ate and drank with their risen Lord (Acts 10:41) during the forty days before the ascension (Acts 1:3; cf. Exod. 24:18).

The occurrence of the resurrection on the morning of the third day is another possible covenantal motif (cf. Exod. 19:11, 16; Hos. 6:2; Gen. 22:4).[15]

The evangelists' predilection for the exodus model has also been claimed as the explanation for the special

---

[14] The statement that Jesus' covenant blood was shed for many for the remission of sins involves further ties with the Sinaitic Covenant via intermediate points in the trajectory: the Jeremianic prophecy of the new (law) covenant (Jer. 31:31) and the Isaianic prophecy of the new (Mosaic) covenant Servant (Isa. 53:12).

[15] Cf. W. Brueggemann, "Amos 4:4-13 and Israel's Covenant Worship," *Vetus Testamentum*, XV (1965), 1-15; J. Wijngaards, "Death and Resurrection in Covenantal Context (Hos. 6:2)," *Vetus Testamentum*, XVII (1967), 226-239.

attention called to the wilderness setting in the accounts of certain highly significant episodes in Jesus' life. The suggestion gains plausibility from the fact that the events themselves are strongly evocative of various features of Israel's wilderness experience following the exodus from Egypt; particularly so are the baptism of Jesus in connection with the activities of John the Forerunner, the forty days temptation of Jesus, and the feeding of the five thousand. If this underscoring of the wilderness setting is indeed designed to set forth Jesus' mission as a new exodus, what needs to be more clearly recognized is that the wilderness of the exodus was above all the place of the covenant-making. It was the place where Yahweh brought Israel into the bond of marriage (Jer. 2:2; Ezek. 16:8; 20:35-37). The highlighting of the wilderness setting of the opening events of Jesus' career thus advises us from the very outset that we are to view his mission as a leading forth of the new Israel-bride to the ratification of the covenant with the Lord, her husband.

We turn now to observe how the authors of the New Testament gospels brought out the Moses-Jesus parallel in their portrayal of Jesus as mediator of the new covenant. The various Moses-like features may be subsumed under the categories of ruler and deliverer, the functions by which Stephen summarized the role of Moses when he too was drawing a parallel between Moses and Christ (Acts 7:35).

As a preface to this functional comparison we will list certain parallels in the literary structure of the records of the personal origins and the calls of these two covenant mediators. This literary parallelism, though not in itself typological, is another indication of the evangelists' design of depicting Jesus as a new Moses. It also enforces quite directly our main thesis concerning the literary relationship of the gospels to the Book of Exodus.

Birth narratives are prominent in the introductions to the accounts of the old and new mediators (Exod. 2:1ff.; Matt. 1:18ff.; Lk. 1:5ff.). They include a statement of the lineage of the child (Exod. 2:1; cf. 1:1ff.; 6:14ff., esp. 20; Matt. 1:1ff.; Lk. 3:23ff.), and the genealogy of Moses continues the genealogical tradition of the Book of Genesis, which is also incorporated into the genealogy of Jesus. These narratives are set within the international political scene of the day and in particular are related to royal decrees that are directed against the life of Israelite infants and thus threaten the destined deliverer of God's people (Exod. 1:15ff.; Matt. 2:16ff.). Interestingly, extensive birth narrative appears again in the Old Testament in the history of Samuel, who, among Old Testament figures after Moses, performed most comprehensively the work of a covenant mediator. And at that point in this literary trajectory from Exodus to the gospels is found the song of praise for Hannah's expected child (1 Sam. 2:1ff.), of which Mary's Magnificat is reminiscent (Lk. 1:46ff.). The birth narratives of both Moses and Jesus also record the naming of the child, and the occasion in each case is evocative of the circumstances of the exodus-deliverance he was later to accomplish (Exod. 2:5-10; Lk. 2:21).[16]

The earlier life of both Moses and Jesus remains largely hidden from view. But in each case an episode is disclosed that was indicative of the future deliverer's sense of vocation and the failure of others to understand the divine purpose (Exod. 2:11ff.; cf. Acts 7:25; Heb. 11:24ff.; Lk. 2:41ff.). The hidden years of preparation issue in both cases in acts of commissioning, attended by special manifestations of God (Exod. 3:1ff.; Matt. 3:16f.; Mk. 1:10f.; Lk. 3:21f.; Jn. 1:32f.). Closely associated with the calls are episodes of personal participation by

[16] In Matthew's account of the flight into Egypt and the return, which he entwines with the birth narratives, he makes an explicit typological connection of the history of Jesus with the exodus by relating the episode to Hosea's observation that God had called his son, the nation Israel, out of Egypt at the time of its national childhood (Matt. 2:15; Hos. 11:1). Compare also Matthew 2:20 and Exodus 4:19.

the two leaders in signs of covenantal judgment (Exod. 4:24ff.; Matt. 3:13ff.; Mk. 1:9ff.; Lk. 3:21f.). The subsequent narratives relate series of miracles performed by or through Moses and Jesus. In each case these are characterized as "signs" and they serve in part to attest the divine authorization of the mediator's mission (Exod. 4:8ff.; 7:3; 8:23; 10:1f.; Jn. 20:30). There are, moreover, striking correspondences in the nature of certain of the signs; compare, for example, the first in each series—Exodus 7:19 and John 2:1ff.

The gospels reveal Jesus engaged in a ministry of deliverance that recalls at several significant points the activity of Moses in delivering Israel. Like Moses, Jesus rescued from hostile, threatening forces. His deliverance of the victims of demon possession from the diabolical powers answered to God's deliverance of Israel from bondage by the hand of Moses; for pharaonic Egypt with its gods is viewed in the Old Testament as the realm of the dragon (Ps. 74:12ff.; Isa. 51:9f.; cf. Ezek. 29:3ff.; 32:2ff.). Jesus' saving of the disciples from stormy seas recalls the exodus salvation at the sea (Matt. 8:24ff.; 14:24ff.), along with other historic displays of the Creator's sovereign control over the chaotic waters. Because the death of Jesus was prefigured in his baptism, in which the water ordeal symbolism of the Red Sea passage was renewed (cf. 1 Cor. 10:1ff.),[17] we may say with biblical propriety that Jesus, like Moses, leads his people through the sea of death.

The figure of shepherd-guide is applied to Jesus and to Moses (Mk. 6:34; cf. Ezek. 34:5ff.; and Ps. 77:20; cf. Num. 27:17). Like Moses, Jesus led his followers, supplying their physical needs, going on before them to the promised rest (Jn. 14:2f.; cf. Matt. 26:32; 28:7). When Jesus spread a table in the wilderness for the thousands, the provision of the manna and other sustenance in the wilderness during the ministry of Moses found a Mes-

[17] See *BOC*, pp. 56ff.

sianic counterpart (Jn. 6:5ff.; cf. Matt. 14:15ff.; Mk. 6:35ff.; Lk. 9:12ff.; and Matt. 15:32ff.; Mk. 8:1ff.).

Central to Jesus' role as deliverer was the ministry of sacrifice and intercession that came to its chief expression in the final stages of his earthly career, the priestly ministry by which he secured acceptance for his people with God. This too answered to a prototype in the service rendered by the mediator of the old covenant. For though the special priestly office was assigned to Aaron and his line, Moses officiated at the covenant sacrifice (Exod. 24:4-8) and engaged in remarkable intercession with God in behalf of jeopardized Israel in the crisis at Sinai (Exod. 32:11ff., 30ff.; 34:8f.; Ps. 106:23; Jn. 17).

Under the heading of Jesus as ruler, his office as mediatorial representative of God before men comes into consideration. In this capacity he inaugurated the covenant and founded the kingdom, organizing the community of faith and promulgating the law of its life and order. Here is the core of the matter for the purposes of the present study and here the new Moses typology of the gospels is crystal clear.

Even when stating the contrast between Moses and Jesus Christ in terms of law over against grace and truth, John draws attention to their common mediatorial role. It was "through" Moses and "through" Christ that the old and new covenants came (Jn. 1:17).

Jesus' identity as the prophet like unto Moses, affirmed by Peter (Acts 3:22f.), is reflected in the gospels (Jn. 5:43; 12:48f.; Matt. 17:5), and the prophetic role of Moses was precisely his role as mediator of the covenant. The prophetic-legislative passage in the Deuteronomic treaty that instituted the office of the prophet defines it as a continuation of the function of Moses at the Sinai covenant-making (Deut. 18:15-19). The prophets of the old covenant down to John the Forerunner were thus primarily covenant messengers, like unto Moses as channels of covenant revelation and as agents of covenant administration. But Jesus Christ was the prophet like

unto Moses in the full sense that he was the mediator-
prophet in the inauguration of the covenant and the
establishment of the kingdom. John stresses the uniqueness of the prophetic vision of the Son: only he has seen
the Father (Jn. 6:46). But even here John may be allud-
ing comparatively to the special intimacy of the vision of
God enjoyed by Moses beyond others in the old economy
(Exod. 33:18ff.; Deut. 34:10; Jn. 1:17f.). Certainly the
transfiguration narrative in the Synoptics (Matt. 17:1ff.;
Mk. 9:2ff.; Lk. 9:28ff.) contains an impressive set of
analogues to the experience of Moses, the prophet-mediator at Sinai. The covenantal perspective is manifested by
the presence of Moses and also of Elijah, whose ministry
of covenant renewal recapitulated so strikingly various
episodes in the life of Moses. The transfiguration tran-
spired on the mountain enveloped by the theophanic
glory cloud. Was it perhaps in part because Peter was so
much under the impression of the similarity of it all to
the Sinai event, which had issued in the establishing of
God's tabernacle among his people, that, still not sufficiently minding the things of God (Matt. 16:23; Mk.
8:33), he came up with the suggestion that the transfiguration occasion might immediately have a similar out-
come—as though Pentecost might come before Jesus had
accomplished his exodus? The voice from heaven commanding, "Hear him," echoed Deuteronomy 18:18, so
designating Jesus as the Moses-like prophet invested with
oracular authority. And the glory shining from the face
of the transfigured Jesus was manifestly the transcendent
counterpart to the reflection of the glory of the Shekinah
that was seen in the face of Moses after he had been in
the mount of the covenant (Exod. 24:15ff.; 34:29ff.; cf.
2 Cor. 3:7ff.).

Also relevant to the gospels' Moses-mediator typology
is the identification of Jesus in the gospels as the Isaianic
Servant of the Lord, for it was the figure of Moses, the
servant of Yahweh in the founding of the Sinaitic Covenant, that Isaiah drew upon in forming the figure of the

Servant whom God would give as a covenant of the people (Isa. 42:6; 49:8).

As ruler of Israel at the inauguration of the covenant, Moses was the human founder of the Old Testament kingdom: he organized the covenant community in its twelve divisions on the basis of the twelve tribal fathers and he communicated to the people the words of God's covenant, the constitution of the kingdom. This model clearly comes into play when the gospels present Jesus as the founder of the kingdom of the new covenant. Jesus gathered and commissioned the twelve to be the apostolic foundation of his church. In his teaching he defined the nature and historical function of his kingdom and set forth the basic principles of its structure and life. The scene of the sermon on the mount, which epitomizes Jesus' authoritative teaching role, recalls unmistakably the figure of Moses at Mount Sinai.

There may be some heuristic value in observing how important strands in the teaching of Jesus fit into the categories of the treaty pattern appropriated in the covenantal writings of Moses.[18] Corresponding to the opening preamble of such treaties, in which the suzerain, speaking in the first person, identifies himself, are Jesus' words of self-identification and especially his "I am" declarations. In all that Jesus said by way of explanation of the Father's redemptive purpose in sending his Son the covenant claims of God upon his people come to expression after the fashion of the reviews of the covenant relationship in the historical prologues of the treaties. And in Jesus' overviews of Israel's history of covenant-breaking, particularly in certain parables such as those of the wicked husbandmen and the marriage of the king's son, we see an adaptation of the historical prologue in the style of the prophetic lawsuit. Treaty stipulations concerning various individual and corporate areas of covenant life find parallels in the instruction given by Jesus.

[18] Cf. above, Part II, Chapters 1 and 2.

Jesus' commandments deal with personal-neighbor relationships, with the authority structure and discipline of the new covenant institution (Matt. 16:18f.; 18:15ff.), and with its ministry of word and sacrament (Matt. 26:26ff.; Mk. 14:22ff.; Lk. 22:19f.; Matt. 28:18ff.). In a manner analogous to the ceremonial legislation of Moses prescribing the symbols of the cultus, the parables of Jesus present the mysteries of the kingdom in a figure. [19] Treaty stipulations were followed by treaty sanctions (cf. Exod. 23:20ff.; Lev. 26; Deut. 28-30). It is this tradition of blessings and curses that is resumed by Jesus in his beatitudes and his threats of doom against offenders (Matt. 5:3ff.; 7:24-27; 23:13ff.). The eschatological discourses of Jesus also stand in continuity with the treaty-sanction tradition as received through the prophetic channel of Old Testament apocalyptic.[20]

In the gospels' accounts of the final stages of Jesus' earthly ministry there are parallels to the life and work of Moses recorded in the Pentateuch beyond the Book of Exodus. The Johannine account of the farewell discourse of Jesus (Jn. 13-17) recalls Moses' Deuteronomic farewell to Israel. In each case it is the hour of covenant ratification. Prominent in the two farewells are similar elements like election of the covenant servants, the Lord-servant relationship, the giving of commandments, the covenant witnesses, and the appointment of a successor for the departing mediator. Both Moses and Jesus make a final disposition through testamentary blessing (Deut. 33) or promise (Jn. 14) and intercession (Jn. 17), bestowing on the community an inheritance of peace, joy, and glory in the unity of the name of the Lord. Subsequently, each covenant mediator takes leave of the earthly scene from the site of a mountain top.

[19] Cf. Matthew 13:10ff.; Mark 4:10ff.; Luke 8:9f. Ezekiel 40-48 is an intermediate development between the cultic legislation and the parable.

[20] Cf. above, pp. 58ff.

It was the task of both the old and new covenant mediators, after defeating the forces of Satan and sealing the covenant of God with his people, to erect the sanctuary house of God. The last chapters of Exodus deal with the construction of the tabernacle under the leadership of Moses and the filling of the finished structure by God's Spirit, visibly present in the form of the cloud of glory (Exod. 40).[21] While the resurrection accounts in the gospels record the raising up of the temple of the new covenant in the sense that Jesus himself is that temple, it is beyond the gospels in the Book of Acts that the further antitypical parallel to the conclusion of the Book of Exodus is found. In the Pentecost-event Christ erects the temple of his church and the Holy Spirit fills the house of God (Acts 2:1ff.).

Parenthetically, it may be noted here that both Exodus and the gospels, though distinct literary entities in themselves, belong (or, in the case of the gospels, may belong) to larger literary units into which their covenant-mediator themes extend. The relation of Exodus to the Mosaic Pentateuch as a whole is formally much the same as that of the Gospel of Luke to the entire Lucan work of Luke-Acts.

Finally, there are new exodus elements in the gospels in which Jesus is presented not as a new Moses but as one who utterly transcends Moses. Jesus, like Moses, provides for his followers and leads them in the way; but Jesus is himself the provision—the true bread from heaven (Jn. 6:35) and water of life (Jn. 4:10ff.; 7:37ff.), and Jesus is the way (Jn. 14:6). Like Moses, Jesus offers the covenant sacrifice, but Jesus is himself that sacrifice. Moses lifted up the serpent on the pole as a symbol of divine judgment; the death of Jesus was that divine judgment in antitypical finality (Jn. 3:14f.; 12:32). Jesus, like Moses, builds the house of God, but Jesus also is himself the

[21] Cf. Meredith M. Kline, "The Holy Spirit as Covenant Witness" (Th.M. dissertation, Westminster Theological Seminary, 1972), pp. 28ff.

temple (Jn. 2:19ff.). Jesus and Moses are both covenant servants of the Lord, but Jesus is at the same time the Lord of all covenant servants. He is the Creator Lord who directs the turbulent waters for the salvation of his covenant people, the Angel of the Lord who leads them in the exodus and through the wilderness, the Lord of the covenant who proclaims with original divine authority the law of the covenant and who, in the day of the Lord, administers the covenant's sanctions, the everlasting curse and blessing (Matt. 25:31ff.).

* * * * *

It needs to be stressed again that, on the one hand, the presence of the exodus typology in the gospels is not in itself direct evidence for regarding the gospels and Exodus as one literary genre and, on the other, that the thesis of this chapter would not be invalidated if some or even all the instances alleged in the preceding section as examples of that typology should be deemed illusory. However, the data actually do show clearly that the gospels make extensive use of this typological model. Although not direct evidence for our thesis, these data do help to demonstrate that the underlying and unifying factor in the portrayal of Jesus' mission in the gospels is his role as mediator of the new covenant and that the controlling and cohesive motif of the passion narratives is the ratification of the new covenant. The prominence given to the exodus typology by the authors of the New Testament gospels discloses an awareness on their part that they stand as Scriptural authors in the line of the transparently covenantal tradition of the Book of Exodus.

Canonical Function of the Gospel Genre

The generic identification of the New Testament gospels with the Book of Exodus has implications for our understanding of the particular canonical function performed by the gospels within the New Testament and thus within the life of the church. For it is a natural assumption that the Lord who authored the covenantal Scriptures will have employed the gospel genre with similar purpose in the canons of the old and new covenants.[22]

The Book of Exodus, itself a by-form of the treaty genre, served a purpose in the Israelite community very much like that of the Mosaic treaty documents themselves. In accordance with procedures followed with Near Eastern treaties, the two tables of the covenant and the Deuteronomic document were deposited before the Lord God in his sanctuary to be objective, legal witnesses to the solemn transaction by which the covenant engagement had been entered upon (Deut. 31:26).[23] Periodically read to the covenant people, the treaty text kept Israel in remembrance of Yahweh's lordly rights and of the sovereign claims his redemptive grace made upon the allegiance of his redeemed people. The oral republishing of the treaty also kept before the people their specific obligations as Yahweh's servants and the accompanying sanctions of the covenant.

In fact, if we are to understand "the book of the law" which Moses placed by the ark (Deut. 31:9, 26; cf. Josh. 24:26; 1 Sam. 10:25) as the entire Pentateuchal corpus, the Book of Exodus would itself be included in the literary deposit to which the function of covenant witness is explicitly attributed. But even if Exodus was not part of the special enshrined covenant documentation, we would be pointed to the same conclusion concerning its purpose in the Old Testament canon by its contents—its dominant account of the ratification of the Sinaitic Covenant and of the establishment of God's rule in the covenant community, set within the broader framework of the narrative of the mission of the covenant mediator.

[22] Cf. above, pp. 45ff., 94ff.
[23] Cf. above, pp. 123ff., 141.

And in either case, as part of Israel's Scriptures, copies of which came to be multiplied in the course of time, the Book of Exodus (and the Pentateuch as a whole) will have performed this witness function in a form more generally available to the people than a document kept in a sanctuary of extremely restricted access.

If then in adopting the gospel genre once again in the administration of the new covenant, the Lord of the covenant designed that the gospels of Matthew, Mark, Luke, and John should perform the same function for the church that the Gospel of Moses performed for Israel, their purpose is to provide documentary attestation to the new covenant. Doubling the number of official documentary witnesses provided for the Sinaitic Covenant (i.e., the two stone tablets), the Lord gave the community of the new covenant four such witnesses, and indeed four different rather than duplicate witnesses as in the case of the Sinaitic tablets.[24]

To provide the legal documentary witness to the historically accomplished fact of the ratification of the new covenant by God's action in the mediatorial mission of Jesus Christ—that is the distinctive function of the four gospels in the canon of the New Testament. This witness function of the gospels is to be distinguished from what is usually in view when the gospels are identified as witness documents, as they often are. The point being made here is not that the gospels are the witness concerning Jesus Christ given to the world by the human authors of the gospels or by the church. The kind of witness we have in mind is not a human witness but a witness of God, the Lord of the covenant. It is not a witness to the world but to the church, the community of God's covenant people. It is not a kerygmatic but a legal witness,[25] not keryg-

[24] Cf. also Deuteronomy 19:15; Matthew 18:16.

[25] Indeed, kerygmatic witness, though distinguishable from legal witness, always has a legal character; it is a witness borne in the name of the Judge of all the earth.

matic-evangelistic proclamation of Jesus Christ but legal attestation to God's covenant.

The gospels are, to be sure, of human as well as divine authorship and are, therefore, a human witness too. [26] Moreover, the gospels obviously do testify to Jesus Christ and proclaim the significance of his saving mission. Certainly, too, their contents are to be used in the church's evangelization of the world. But when we consider the structure and the total contents of the gospels, particularly their dominant concern with covenant ratification, and especially when we view the matter in the light of the equivalency of the gospels to the Book of Exodus, we are brought to the conclusion that the specific canonical function of the gospels is to be defined from the perspective of God's use of them as legal documents in the administration of his covenant.

Understood as covenant ratification witnesses, the gospels have a breadth of purpose that accounts fully for all their contents. It is unnecessary to make a choice, as is usually done, between classifying the gospels as primarily lives of Jesus or as church manuals of one sort or another. The problem thus posed is false and a solution in either direction is bound to be one-sided and inadequate. The covenant reality and the treaty structure, of which the gospels of the old and new covenants are a by-form, provide the comprehensive framework of theological concept and literary pattern within which both types of material, history of Jesus data and community instruction, find their full and proper explanation. The gospels' particular range of subject matter is altogether natural and authentic within the tradition of covenant witness documents.

To define the nature and purpose of the gospels in

---

[26] The conscious and express purpose of this human witness to authenticate the historical accomplishment of God's covenant program (cf. Lk. 1:1ff.) is clearly in complete congruity with what we have determined to be the purpose of the gospels as divine witnesses.

covenantal rather than Christological terms is not to depreciate the significance of Jesus but simply to recognize the specific focus of the Christology of the gospels within their broader covenantal perspective. Certainly there is no tension of interests between the lord of a covenant and his covenant. The covenant documents are precisely the instruments by which a suzerain reveals and enforces his authoritative will. They are exponential of lordship.

That is especially true of the treaty preamble. In the biblical adaptation of the treaty form, the preamble is the revelation of the name of God as Lord of the covenant. This revelation of God's name not only points to the source and foundation of the covenant reality but is itself the ultimate objective of the covenant relationship. And in the gospels, identified as covenantal documents, the Christology performs this supremely significant preamble-like function. It proclaims the name of Jesus, the Lord of the covenant, revealing him as God present with his people, the primary reality of God's covenant relationship to man, and as Savior of his people, the central reality of the redemptive covenant relationship. The covenantal orientation given to Christology in the gospels does not, therefore, detract from its importance but rather enhances it. The kerygmatic impact of the Christology is actually strengthened, for the revelation of the name of Jesus comes in its treaty preamble capacity as a sovereign summons to covenantal commitment, the commitment of believing discipleship under Jesus as sign-attested mediator of the covenant (Jn. 20:31; cf. Exod. 4:1ff.; 14:31), indeed as covenant Lord and God.

At the same time, the gospels' preamble-like revelation of the Lord of the covenant is such as to show the wisdom and even necessity of defining the gospel genre in terms broader than Christology. For they reveal the covenant Lord by the name of Father and by the name of Spirit as well as by the name of Son. Their theology proper is not narrowly Christological and it is an advantage of the broader identification of the gospels as documents of covenant certification that it can accommodate this more broadly theological character of the texts.

A breadth of perspective along with a centrality of emphasis on Jesus Christ, similar to what we have posited for the gospel documents, is present in the meaning of the word "gospel" (*euangelion*) as it is used in the New Testament gospels. Though this usage is relevant to our present purposes, it does not have as direct a bearing as one might think on the definition of the gospels as documents, since in the evangelists' usage the word does not refer to the documents as such but rather to their central message, the good tidings proclaimed by Jesus and by his followers.

This gospel message is indeed characterized as a message about Jesus Christ (Mk. 1:1), but more comprehensively it is designated "the gospel of the kingdom" (Matt. 4:23; 9:35; 24:14; Mk. 1:14f.). In the Old Testament antecedents of the terminology of heralding the good tidings, those tidings refer prophetically to the reign of the Lord God in the Messianic age, to the coming of the Lord to his people in glory to rule with power and justice, rendering to each his recompense (cf. Isa. 40:9; 52:7ff.; 60:6; 61:1).

The coming of the kingdom of God announced by the gospel tidings is very much the same event as the inauguration of God's covenant. For a divine covenant "is a sovereign administration of the kingdom of God. Covenant administration is kingdom administration."[27] The establishment of the covenant order is the coming of God to dwell enthroned in a reign of salvation among his people. Therefore, to say the New Testament gospels testify to the ratification of the new covenant is tantamount to saying that they declare the arrival of the age of God's kingdom. It is to say that the gospel documents certify the gospel tidings. Since the gospel tidings, like

27 *BOC,* p. 36.

the gospel documents that contain and certify them, are concerned with the broadly theological theme of the kingdom and covenant of God, the adoption of the label "gospels" for the documents themselves, which evidently occurred in the second century A.D., was quite appropriate, particularly since the term covenant (or testament) came to designate the New Testament canon as a whole.

The witness of the gospels certifying that God had fulfilled his ancient covenant oath (cf. Gen. 15; Deut. 32:40ff.) by establishing the new covenant through his Son is a divine witness. In the gospels, God himself bears witness. More specifically, the divine gospel-witness documents are the witness of God the Spirit to the covenant as now ratified and the kingdom as now realized.

The Scriptures attribute to the Spirit of God the role of divine witness at the making of the Sinaitic Covenant. To appreciate the significance of the relevant biblical data it is first necessary to observe that it is the Spirit in particular who is identified with the theophanic pillar of the glory-cloud (cf., e.g., Isa. 63:11ff.; Hag. 2:5; Neh. 9:19f.).[28] One passage, Haggai 2:5, is of special interest in this regard because it specifically identifies the Spirit with the theophanic pillar functioning as covenant witness. The prophet encourages the people in the rebuilding of the house of God by giving them God's assurance of his presence with them (v. 4b) and of the ultimate completion of his house, which will take place in connection with a new exodus-despoiling of Egypt and a new Sinaitic shaking of the earth (vv. 6ff.). As a support for their confidence in the certain consummation of the covenant, the Lord calls their attention to the divine validation of the covenant relation at Sinai. He reminds them in particular of his treaty word and also of his own visible presence there as a divine witness to the covenant in the form of the glory-pillar: "This is what I covenanted [literally,

---

[28] For the evidence in full, see M. M. Kline, op. cit.; for the Spirit's covenant-witness function, see pp. 56ff.

the word I cut] with you, when you came out of Egypt, when my Spirit stood in your midst" (v. 5). Unfortunately, the allusion is lost in the usual versions, which turn the last clause of verse 5 into a statement that the Spirit abode among the Israelites in Moses' day, or, worse still, that the Spirit was abiding among Haggai's contemporaries. The allusion to the Sinaitic pillar of glory, however, is clear. The verb in verse 5b (*'āmad*) is the verb used to describe the glory-pillar as standing in Israel's midst (Exod. 14:19; 33:9f.). In fact, the noun "pillar" (*'ammûd*) is derived from this verbal root. The symbolic significance of the pillar form of the theophany may be gathered from the fact that pillars of various kinds served as witness objects for a variety of legal transactions. [29] The pillar form of the Spirit's manifestation thus reveals that he was present at Sinai in the capacity of witness to the covenant.

The Spirit also functioned as covenant witness at Sinai by way of the documentary witnesses of the Sinaitic Covenant, for it was the Spirit of God who, as the Spirit of prophecy, inspired the composition of the covenant documents. Moreover, the divine agency in the actual inscribing of the two stone tablets of covenant witness is said to have been "the finger of God" (Exod. 31:18; cf. 8:19), and Scripture elsewhere equates "the finger of God" and the Spirit.[30] This situation illuminates and is in turn illuminated by 2 Corinthians 3:3, which evidently attributes to the Spirit the writing of the tables of stone.

As the Holy Spirit performs his witness function once again in the divine administration of the new covenant, the phenomena of his coming at Pentecost and his miraculous working in the apostolic church are similar in mode and purpose to his manifestation and wonders in the case of the Sinaitic Covenant. [31] But what is of most immedi-

---

[29] *Ibid.*, pp. 60f.

[30] *Ibid.*, pp. 52ff. Compare Luke 11:20 with Matthew 12:28.

[31] *Ibid.*, pp. 8ff.

ate interest for our analysis of the gospels is the correspondence between the Spirit's activity as divine Inspirer
and primary Author of the gospels and his writing of the
two stone tablets and inspiring of the canonical witness
documents of the old covenant.

Authored by the Spirit, the gospels are the witness of
God the Spirit to the historical inauguration of the new
covenant through Jesus Christ and to the basic terms of
the covenant—its organizational regulations and programmatic commission for the church, its fundamental religious and ethical norms, and its eschatological sanctions.
"He that hath an ear, let him hear what the Spirit saith
unto the churches."

INDEXES

I. Index of Scripture References

II. Index of Names and Subjects

III. Index of Authors